INCLUSIVE SPONSORSHIP

INCLUSIVE SPONSORSHIP

A Bold Vision to Advance Women of Color in the Workplace

JHAYMEE TYNAN

ROWMAN & LITTLEFIELD
Lanham • Boulder • New York • London

Published by Rowman & Littlefield
An imprint of The Rowman & Littlefield Publishing Group, Inc.
4501 Forbes Boulevard, Suite 200, Lanham, Maryland 20706
www.rowman.com

86-90 Paul Street, London EC2A 4NE

British Library Cataloguing in Publication Information Available

Library of Congress Cataloging-in-Publication Data

Names: Tynan, Jhaymee, 1981– author.
Title: Inclusive sponsorship : a bold vision to advance women of color in
    the workplace / Jhaymee Tynan.
Description: Lanham : Rowman & Littlefield, [2022] | Includes
    bibliographical references and index.
Identifiers: LCCN 2022010565 (print) | LCCN 2022010566 (ebook) | ISBN
    9781538160398 (cloth) | ISBN 9781538160404 (epub)
Subjects: LCSH: Career development. | Executives—Training of. | Minority
    women—Employment. | Diversity in the workplace.
Classification: LCC HF5549.5.C35 T96 2022 (print) | LCC HF5549.5.C35
    (ebook) | DDC 658.3/124082—dc23/eng/20220307
LC record available at https://lccn.loc.gov/2022010565
LC ebook record available at https://lccn.loc.gov/2022010566

This book is dedicated to my nieces, Aviana and Alana. May you always find the courage, strength, and support to go after your dreams.

Surround yourself with women that would mention your name in a room full of opportunities.

—Anonymous

CONTENTS

PREFACE

Writing a book was never a goal of mine, nor was it a career aspiration. I didn't major in English as an undergrad, and I always thought that writing a book was a career choice for fulltime authors or people who had amazing life stories. I didn't realize how important a book could be, how it could inspire others to act. I knew if I wrote a book, I wanted the book to not only be helpful for the reader but also to give him or her a different perspective on how they can make an impact. I toyed with the idea of writing a book for about two years, encouraged by colleagues and friends, and I remember just where I was when the idea was planted in my mind.

I had taken time off from work to attend a national women's conference for two main reasons. The first was to escape my work environment. It had been three months since I had experienced being bullied by my direct manager, and I needed a reprieve from the daily stress and fear that I felt every time I stepped into my office. The second reason was that I was desperately looking for my next job. I was in a very negative space and needed some time to clear my mind about what I wanted to do in the next chapter of my life. I jumped into my car and drove six hours through the mountains to Nashville, Tennessee, in the pouring rain thinking about how I could change my career outcomes. Throughout the entire drive, I tried to downplay negative talk, quieting my inner imposter, and looking forward to the next two days, where I could network and shed all the negativity that was currently clouding my ability to focus. I couldn't believe I was in this place mentally, especially after all of the good things I experienced that year. Two months prior I had married and went on a fantastic honeymoon. Around that same time, I was honored by the *Charlotte Business Journal* as being one of the 40 under 40 honorees for accomplishments in my professional and personal life. And hours before I got on a plane to Miami for my Cuban-style intimate wedding, I found out that I had been elected to my first national board of directors. Things were going pretty well, but in the weeks that followed, I had experienced intimidation, retaliation, and backbiting from a female leader whom at one time in my career I admired. To say that this women's conference was a reprieve is a complete understatement. I have never looked forward to a professional conference more. I saw it as an opportunity to explore my options, expand my connections, and have a few days completely to myself for thoughtful introspection.

I sat down in one of the first sessions, where speakers from McKinsey and Lean In were reviewing the statistics of women's advancement in the workplace. I was excited to hear the report and was interested in how I could take the data back to my organization to help with advancing women, and specifically women of color, in my field. As the statistics flashed across the slides, I felt myself getting more and more frustrated. Similar data points around the percentage of Black women in leadership roles and the amount of money Latina women make dollar per dollar compared to their white male counterparts seemed all too familiar. It felt eerily like déjà vu, as if I'd heard the story before in the years prior. Here we were in 2018, and we still hadn't seen the outcomes around diversifying leadership that we continue to talk about in these forums. Every year, we come together at major conferences. We exchange business cards. We eat amazing food and drink delicious cocktails. We smile and we discuss how frustrating and disappointing it is that we keep having to have this conversation around women's advancement. Yet the statistics remain unchanged.

About twenty-five minutes into the presentation, my blood was boiling. I sat there, staring at the slides and listening to the speaker provide several tactics to improve the advancement of women in corporate America. There it was. The slides included the same tactics I had seen at other conferences and heard in podcasts and read in blog articles from experts and thought leaders in the diversity and inclusion space. Here we go again, I thought. Who will have the courage and bravery to take these tactics and put them into action? I looked around the room, and audience members both male and female were furiously scribbling down notes and nodding their heads about what they were hearing. Several were senior leaders in their organizations, some even CEOs. It looked like a wave of bobbing heads, but a paralyzed wave of bobbing heads.

I too was scribbling down notes, a series of bullet points on the data I'd heard and then one question that I posed to myself. Who is going to fix this? Who is going to take action so that next year we might actually see some improvement in these numbers? I even thought about my own organization where these statistics rang true. My blood continued to boil feverishly. I thought about all the talented women of color I'd come across in my organization who had been either passed up for promotions, or perhaps never considered asking for promotion. Yet, our white colleagues continue to thrive through awards, recognition, promotions, and support to be thought leaders on the national stage. Don't get me wrong. Many of my white colleagues deserve those accolades, and I certainly am supportive when they achieve success. But so many of my Black, Indigenous, People of Color (BIPOC) colleagues deserve accolades and success as well.

The session ended, and we poured out into the lobby for a quick coffee break before the next series of activities. I had so many thoughts and questions swirling around in my head. Again, I thought, who is going to fix this? We know that lack of representation is an issue at many companies and many consulting firms, and think tanks have provided us with specific tactics that we can readily employ to move in the right direction. As I sipped my third cup of coffee that morning, I felt myself getting angrier at all of the executives sitting in the room who had the power, influence, and authority to do the right thing. I remember pointing my mental finger directly at them and thinking, this is your problem. You caused this. And you have the ability to change it, and yet you will leave this conference and do absolutely nothing. We will be back here again next year with the same information, and you'll be nodding again in agreement but unwilling to take action. Perhaps it was that I was already in the negative space. Perhaps I had pent-up rage based on my experience at work and I wanted to use the executives in the room as an invisible punching bag for how I was feeling at the time. Whatever it was, it caught me by surprise just how upset and uninspired I was from that session.

I took an extended break from those sessions, mainly because my feet were already hurting from the Louboutin shoes I had purchased (er, overextended my budget) for this event. I continued to sip my coffee and reflect. Because I am a problem solver and not one to complain incessantly, I started thinking about what I personally could do to solve this problem. Honestly, even though I had an executive title, I never thought of myself as an executive. I didn't believe that I had the power and influence to be a change maker. Again, more than likely because of my current work environment, I believed less of myself than outsiders looking in. While I never sought the help of a therapist, looking back at that time, I believe that I was clinically depressed. That week alone I had dropped twelve pounds due to lack of eating and lack of restful sleep as I had continual trepidation about my daily interactions with my manager at work. On more than one occasion, she made me feel small. In fact, she had told me that my colleagues at work didn't believe I had any subject matter expertise and that she felt I was undeserving of any recognition or praise for the work I had done for her and the team in the past two and a half years. I think a small part of me started to believe that. So, when I was thinking about what I could do to solve this problem around diversity and leadership, I didn't think I was equipped or had the right professional title or even the right skills to make an impact. Who would listen to me? Who would think that this was something I could solve on my own? Why do I think I'm the right person to solve this problem? I was so taken by these thoughts of inadequacy coupled with the frustration that women like myself continue to have challenges in getting to the next level that I didn't take advantage of all of the opportunities available to me at this conference. I remember driving those six hours back home, not only being afraid to go back to the office, but also angry with myself for not having used that time to start planting the seeds for the next chapter of my life.

Then something magical happened. I don't know if it was fatigue from work or encouragement from my husband or the fact that I wanted to take my career into my own hands and protect my personal and professional brand, but I was sitting upstairs in our media room having received another inflammatory email from my boss, and I said enough was enough. I reached out to a senior leader I had developed a strong working relationship with and asked for advice on how I should navigate the situation I was currently in. After a forty-minute conversation, she sprang into action. She asked me what I was interested in doing for my next steps, and I said there was a high-profile project that I would love to lead if given the opportunity. Within two weeks of that conversation, she had moved me into the lead role for this project, and I was directly reporting to her. Seven months later, I was promoted to assistant vice president and shortly thereafter received a national award from *Modern Healthcare* as one of twenty-five top emerging leaders in healthcare. This was sponsorship personified. It was a senior leader taking action on behalf of the career of a rising leader and having tangible results. It was this moment that provided so much clarity for me on what my purpose in my career truly is. It also became the catalyst for this book.

At the end of 2019, I decided to take action myself. No longer was I concerned that I wasn't a senior leader or that I didn't have power or influence. I had experienced a moment in my career where I took action and mobilized my allies to advance myself and protect my brand. I thought about the many women of color who experience corporate bullying or stifled careers, who have never even heard of what career sponsorship is. And I certainly didn't want to just dip my toe in these waters. I wanted to make a huge splash and prove that no action was too big or too small to advocate for the careers of others. I put pen to paper and wrote an article about my experience and being sponsored, how it impacted me, and how that experience served as inspiration for my values and career goals. I decided to make a public commitment to sponsor one hundred women of color in healthcare by 2030. I knew it was a big, hairy, audacious goal and that it was possible that I would never achieve it. But if I, as one individual, could commit to and achieve sponsorship for one hundred women of color in my industry, then no other executive could claim that it was impossible. It would be a way to hold leaders and executives accountable for lifting up the next generation while achieving tangible results. I wanted to change the narrative around the advancement of women of color. Women of color don't need more mentors. I know this is a controversial thing to say and one that is always cited at conferences as being the approach to giving women of color more exposure and guidance on their career. However, it is my belief that women of color are over-mentored and under-sponsored. The pipeline of women of color exists in almost every organization. You just have to be willing to make the bold decisions to unapologetically promote BIPOC women. Advancing women of color is not a pipeline issue. It's a sponsorship issue.

ACKNOWLEDGMENTS

Writing a book, during a pandemic, was unfathomable without the love and support of my husband, Brian. He gave me the uninterrupted space to journal and write and stood by me when I had bouts of writer's block or when I needed that extra energy to power through. He has been an amazing life partner.

To Minda Harts, thank you for paving the way for people like me to write books from our authentic lived experiences as Black women. Taking your writer's retreat in 2020 was the highlight of my year and gave me the courage to write my first book. I treasure your coaching and your friendship.

To Stephan A. Hart, you have been a tremendous cheerleader and coach as I developed my personal brand and put myself out there on LinkedIn and other social media. I am now more confident in who I am as a leader.

To Gayle Capozzalo, you were the first true sponsor in my career. You have championed me, nominated me for opportunities to share my perspectives, and continue to always be there for me in both mentorship and sponsorship. Thank you for modeling the way.

To Carol Lovin, I share our story of sponsorship because without you, I know that I wouldn't be where I am today. You saw my potential and put me in high-visibility roles that allowed me to step further into my leadership. I am eternally grateful for your courage, bravery, and friendship.

To the 2018 Thomas C. Dolan Executive Diversity Program Cohort, Nichole Wilson, Nicole Radford, E. J. Imafidon, Bini Varughese, and Bruce Chan, thank you for being such a great support system no matter where we all end up in our careers. I cannot wait to see your future successes. Lots of love to each of you.

To My Sister Circle, Priya Bathija, Kate Liebelt, Catherine Carle, Victoria Lee, thank you for giving me the space to laugh, cry, and celebrate our wins together.

To my family. To my father, Chester Wilson Jr., who was the first to believe in my potential and always stands by me no matter what. To my brother, Chester Wilson III, and my sister, Jasmin Wilson, thank you for never making me feel like an imposter and believing that I can achieve all of my dreams. To my mother, Vanessa Wilson, who is reading this book from heaven, thank you for instilling in me a sense of independence and showing me how to lead with both my head and my heart.

I am forever indebted to Tamar Rydzinski, who took a chance on a new author who has dreams of writing leadership books as well as young adult novels. Thank you for helping me get my first book published.

To Suzanne at Rowman & Littlefield publishers, thank you for editing my book and making it the best it could be, and for your grace during the pandemic to get it finished on time.

Finally, to all those who have been a part of my journey: Melissa Davis, Calandra Branch, Andrea Swann, Doug Riddle, Nicole Jones, Nisha Pasupuleti, Layla Ramirez, Camille Strickland, Kinsey Evans, Anika Gardenhire, Keisha Brickham, Alana Cheeks-Lomax, Sophie Zeinu, Wendy Fu, Nicole Bates, Lynn Belvitt, Dr. Deepa Desai, Michael O'Brien, Laurie Cooke, Cie Armstead, Tony Awojoodu, Jasmine Ballard, Lauren Barrow, Jackie Berkey, Morgan Best, Mara Burdick, Jason Byrd, Charlotte Chandler, Oluoma Chukwu, Dr. Alisahah Jackson, Monifa Drayton, Terri Flood, Fran Fredane-Fraser, Sarah Gornto, Modena Henderson, Shayla Higginbotham, Morgan Hinton, Katie Kaney, Jessica Lackey, Marque Macon, Brian Middleton, Stephanie Morgan, Brandi Newman, Nehemie Owen, Kelly Page, Ruth Portacci, Jangar Richards, Lisa Schiller, Tim Stroman, Tracie Taylor, Judit Tejeda, LeVelton Thomas, Toshka Nelson, Alisha Wallace-Smith, Dana Weston Graves, Jon-Michael Williams, Ruth Williams-Brinkley, and Aisha Williams.

1

YOU NEED TO CALM DOWN

Sunshine, crisp autumn weather, the smell of bacon. These were the three phrases I had written in my gratitude journal on my iPad on October 17, 2019. As part of a yearlong coaching journey, I decided to start one, and it had become a comfort and a place of reflection for me as I was fighting my inner demons about my career progression. On one of my many frequent trips for work, I downloaded an audiobook called *The Gratitude Diaries*, by Janice Kaplan, and listened to it straight through. I was enthralled by it. It never occurred to me to think of my life in terms of gratitude. I had spent much of my professional career thinking about all the deficits. I would think about all of the promotions I was passed over for. I would think about the opportunities that were given to other people that I felt weren't as deserving as I was. I would lament the micro aggressions that seemed to enter my day like daggers, whether from a colleague surprised by the fact that I had two master's degrees or from a senior leader who commented astonishingly on how eloquently I spoke. I did not fully appreciate how shifting my mindset from anger to gratitude could have such a positive impact on my leadership style and how I engaged with others. I made my morning coffee and sat with those three phrases for about fifteen minutes before packing a suitcase to drive five hours to Macon, Georgia, for several team meetings for my latest integration project. I laughed internally about how something as trivial as the smell of bacon could euphorically lift me out of a low-grade depression about my career and give me a boost of energy as if I had just guzzled down an energy drink. Several minutes passed before a notification popped up on my phone. It was a text from one of my mentees that wanted to talk urgently. I finished packing, sipped my last bit of Dunkin' Donuts breakfast blend, and headed for my car to give her a call.

When I called her, I heard the pain in her voice. In fact, the few first moments of the call were a bit silent. I could hear her sigh on the other end of the line, as if she had just been crying uncontrollably but trying to catch her breath. When she found her words, she said to me, "I can't take this anymore. I need to find a new job where I feel valued—where my brain is valued." My mentee worked at one of the largest healthcare systems in the country, specifically in the area of population health. She had spent her career developing strategies for local communities on how to improve the health and well-being of underserved populations in urban environments. Her situation was all too common. She had a lot of innovative ideas that would push the organization to think differently about the services it provides in a bold and disruptive way. To me, she is the next generation of healthcare leadership. She has dual degrees, an MHA and a JD from top universities, and is well respected among her peers. By background, she is Indian American and identifies as being a woman of color. Not only is she very ambitious, but she also has very high emotional intelligence (EQ) and is insanely curious about different ways to deliver healthcare and how to fix our broken healthcare system in the United States. A year and a half prior, she had been selected for one of the coveted fellowship positions at her organization and had been identified as being high potential.

Her reporting relationship recently changed due to a redesign of the organization, and she was now reporting to a woman who felt threatened by her expertise. Of course, her boss never outright admitted her insecurities, but her actions demonstrated her shortcomings, nonetheless. My mentee felt that her ideas were being hijacked, her thought leadership was being stolen, and other associates on her team were being amplified and lifted up without having demonstrated high performance. She continued on the call, describing a meeting that she had led with the senior-most executives in her organization that went very well. Her boss did not acknowledge this fact and even went so far as to downplay the work that she did at the team meeting the next day. The icing on the cake was that as her boss was downplaying her work, she was lifting up another colleague's work that wasn't nearly of the same caliber. And let me not forget to mention the dynamics of race at play here. Both her boss and her colleagues are white. My mentee also observed that her colleagues were getting mentored by her boss. She felt that she was being overlooked for those same mentoring opportunities along with the fact that her work and deliverables continued to be viewed as subpar within her team but lauded by other executives throughout the organization. The tension within her team was palpable. Like so many women of color I mentor, my mentees have felt that they work harder and deliver higher quality than their peers, but don't get the same or more respect.

We stayed on the phone for an hour and a half of my drive. Let me say one thing for context. I am not the type of mentor to sugarcoat and not be direct about ways to move forward when you feel that you are not valued by your organization. I gave her several options, which included having a direct conversation with her boss that detailed specific instances of feeling undervalued. I also very directly instructed her to consider developing an exit strategy. Clearly, this experience was having an emotional toll on her, and she could not be her best self if she was continually dealing with the emotional tax of her lived experiences as a woman of color at her organization. Now, please do not misunderstand my counsel as telling rising women of color leaders that they should run away from situations such as this. The tragedy is that this is a very common lived experience for many of us. Usually, these experiences are blanketed by gaslighting and self-doubt that tells us that what we experience is a factor of not only lack of mentorship and sponsorship but also institutionalized racism. It is and continues to be exhausting, especially if you have high ambitions and a vision of how to fulfill them. Sometimes, your personal peace and well-being supersede your need to stay in an organization that doesn't value your knowledge, skills, and abilities. For my mentee, an exit strategy made the best sense because I knew there were organizations that would give her the space and the support to thrive. Fast-forward eighteen months; she left that organization and has been promoted twice to her first junior executive role with increased scope and scale in her responsibilities. She engaged me as her mentor, and I coached and sponsored her through the application and interviewing process—providing her with tactics and tips she should use to highlight her leadership strengths and quantitative skills. She mobilized one of her other close sponsors to advocate for her role as director of population health. That same sponsor fought for her to get the role and the compensation she needed to make the transition. Now, she is on a fast trajectory to continue growing as a healthcare executive and leader.

This story is so essential to understanding the fundamental challenge women of color face when advocating for themselves and climbing the corporate ladder. There is an emotional burden that we must deal with of inequity and competition when trying to get the same promotions and opportunities as our white colleagues. And we must manage our emotions with greater intent than our white colleagues and male colleagues as well. This emotional tax that we bear only makes it more difficult to stay invested in the long haul for our career journeys.

THE EMOTIONAL TAX

If emotions are what make us uniquely human, then why are emotions forbidden in the office? I will freely admit that I am both stubborn and the type of person that typically leads with her heart rather than her head. My grandmother used to sit me down during one of our many one-on-one talks over coffee and say "Jhaymee, you have to stop wearing your heart on your sleeve." I have learned throughout my career to manage my emotions in a way that allows me to still be my authentic self without having to apologize for being emotional, especially in situations that warrant it. Executives should display more emotions in their work because it allows the individuals you lead to know that you are a human being, that you are fallible, and that you are passionate about the things you care about. When I think about the people I have worked for, those leaders who were unafraid to show emotion were the ones I respected most. Being an emotive leader is a unique trait that is not commonly found in leaders in today's world. We are all cautioned against being emotional in the office, when in fact it is that very emotion that can make a leader stronger.

There are two times over the past seventeen years of working where I remember being emotional. One was in my early career in the banking industry, fresh out of four years of undergrad at Virginia Tech. I was missing my sales targets for the upcoming quarter, and I went into a colleague's office and cried uncontrollably. Maybe it was the stress of the situation, or maybe it was the fact that it was the first time in my life where I felt like I truly failed at something, but it was waterworks through and through. I was crying so hard that not only could my team see me crying (we had glass office walls) but also the customers coming in to do their banking. Sure, at the time it felt really good to let out that stress, but I knew that I would never be able to live down the fact that I cried in the office. I chatted with one of my informal mentors later on that day about my experience. Of course, he said everything would be fine. However, I knew I had committed a mortal sin by letting down my guard and unleashing a flurry of tears and anguish at not performing to my absolute best potential.

The second time I was emotional in the workplace happened a couple of years ago, well into my career in healthcare. I was dealing with a stressful situation at work, one that I had never encountered before and would change the trajectory of my career. The team, environment, and culture were so stressful and toxic that I regularly had to shut the door to my office and meditate for about thirty minutes during my lunch break before I could reemerge. My team was under a deadline for a senior-level report, and unfortunately, my leader at the time was not providing the right level of direction as to what she expected. After several rounds of edits, inflammatory emails, and mental pivots, the entire team continued to flounder. The lack of leadership and self-awareness from my former boss was so infuriating that I needed daily therapy sessions. On one particularly "hot mess express" day, I opened the Calm app on my iPhone and completed three consecutive meditation sessions before I believed I could be fully functional for the rest of the day. Had you walked by my office, you would even have heard me blasting "Show Me What You Got" by Jay-Z, one of the songs that give me energy when I need it most. I was constantly trying to relieve myself of negative energy in the most positive ways possible. In both of those instances, I had this feeling of not wanting to be perceived a certain way in the office because I was a Black woman. I often wondered if my white colleagues went through the same mental gymnastics around displaying emotion in the office and how that would be received by their colleagues. I also know that I was very fixated on not wanting to be labeled as angry or emotional or any of the other adjectives that are used in a negative way to describe a passionate woman.

At this point in my career, I realized that how I behaved factored into my future potential in my organization. It was not simply the quality of my work, but how I was being perceived by others. I have friends and colleagues, many of whom are women of color, that talked about this moment in their career: the moment they had to shelter their emotions because of their fear of their team's and their leader's perceptions. This is frequently the point in a woman's career where she starts to truly dissect her behaviors and believe that there is more to getting ahead than her performance. I learned that lesson after only three years in the workforce, and I knew that who I was and the way I looked at that would play a pivotal role in my ability to convince others to believe in and see my potential. Now that I am almost twenty years in the workforce, the story is still the same. The only difference is that I have had mentors and sponsors guiding me along the way and encouraging me to be my authentic self in all situations. But when you don't have a mentor, and most importantly a sponsor, who can dispel the myth surrounding your knowledge, skills, and abilities, the uphill battle will continue to be steep.

THE CALL

It was mid-evening on a regular Thursday night during a particularly brisk fall season. Typically, I have several after-work engagements, receptions, and dinners to attend. I just returned home from one of those events when I looked at my phone and saw that a good friend and colleague of mine, Anne, had texted and wanted to talk about her recent transition. Anne identifies as an African American woman, and we have bonded over the past several years on our mutual affection for horror films, self-help books, and trashy reality television. I hadn't spoken to her in several months, and I had been thinking about her because I knew that she was unhappy in her job. She was a highly respected and well-known thought leader in healthcare, had a national brand, and was making important moves to elevate herself in our industry. I gave her a call and we spent about forty-five minutes talking about her decision to leave her current organization. She worked in management consulting and was on the partner track, which required a lot of travel and consultative selling to demonstrate her readiness for promotion. She was working hard to build her business portfolio and demonstrate her ability to be an equity partner at a very well-respected, global consulting firm. As Anne continued to describe her thoughts and feelings about leaving her job, there was one particular story she shared that rocked me to my core. She described her annual performance review, the one time of year that everyone in consulting dreads the most. She had been advocating for herself and building her business case for promotion over the past eight months and thought that she had support from various other partners, junior to senior, for a promotion to senior manager. She had testimonials from prior clients that she had worked with along with feedback from her teammates; all of that suggested she was a stellar, top performer.

She received a debriefing from her counselor shortly after the annual review meetings concluded, and it was clear from that discussion that she would not be getting promoted that year. When she asked why, her counselor simply said that she did not have the full support of the partnership team for the promotion, and that no one else in the meeting could speak intelligently enough about her experiences and her client work to make her a suitable candidate for that next level. I could hear the dismay and sadness in her voice as she was talking about the countless coffee meetings, golf outings, and dinners that she attended to campaign for the promotion. She thought that she had done all that she could to secure her sponsors before the performance reviews started. At one point during the call, she was speaking so fast and was so flustered that I remember telling her, "Honey, you need to calm down." As it turned out, the individuals that she thought would be part of her performance review were not included, and the individuals that ended up on her review panel were unfamiliar with her work and unwilling to do the due diligence required to ensure that they had a good perspective on her work. She was mentally, physically, and spiritually exhausted and decided that she wanted to become an entrepreneur and go into business for herself. Listening to a woman who is so accomplished and renowned give up her dream of one day becoming an equity partner at her firm simply because of lack of sponsorship was heartbreaking.

These stories are all too common for women of color in a variety of different industries. We spend so much time developing our expertise and "playing the game" only to be met with anguish when lacking the advocacy of leadership to pound the tables for us and our potential within the organization. I cannot tell you how many times I have spoken to former colleagues and acquaintances that had similar interactions with their boss or other senior leaders in their organization. They have been told that although they have amassed strong education, credentials, and experience, they are still not ready for next-level leadership. The challenge and sorrow come when those leaders are asked pointed questions about the reason why these women of color aren't ready, and the answers are ambiguous, leaving them to feel unsupported, untrusting, and small. Common responses from "you just need to work here a little longer and pay your dues" to "no one knows what you do for the organization" are empty pieces of feedback that lack substance. I was once told that I needed to work on my "executive presence" without any specifics on what about my presence needed work. The feedback doesn't feel genuine or actionable because it is not accompanied by tactics or resources to close those performance gaps. Instead, it is used as a stall tactic or a deflection, usually enveloped by institutionalized racism or unconscious bias. The one element that's missing to amplify the careers of women of color is true advocacy—sponsors that are willing to promote them based on their potential and not simply their performances. This was evident in my call with Anne, and it is even more evident with the mentees and protégés I work with daily. Women of color are left to navigate their careers on their own. Getting lost in the shuffle is a very real phenomenon that happens when we try to advance our careers without sponsorship.

MY INFLECTION POINT

My inflection point came at the hands of a bully in the workplace. I had never been made to feel so small in my entire life as when my former boss was sitting across the table from me and explaining to me why she felt that I was undeserving of a recent recognition I had received, based on my work project for the past two and a half years. She went on about how she felt that I was overselling my skills and that the scope of my role was not worthy of national recognition. In the room was a member of the HR department who sat quietly listening to the conversation and taking a few notes here and there as she looked at each of us trying to understand the dynamics that were unfolding before her. I sat there, biting my tongue, trying desperately to prevent myself from leaning into the angry Black woman stereotype or showing emotion of any kind. My head was swirling in a thousand directions, dealing with trying to remain poised and in control, but boiling inside, thinking of the audacity she had to make me feel like I was nothing. The meeting lasted a total of thirty minutes, but it felt like I was in there for an eternity. At the end of the meeting, she looked at me and asked me to come up with an action plan of how I was going to improve all of the relationships damaged from receiving this national recognition. I remember thinking to myself how ironic it was to be asked to put together a plan to improve relationships from a person who lacked credibility, authenticity, and genuine kindness. I went back to my office, closed the door, and exhaled.

I sent a text message to one of my closest girlfriends in my sister circle, a group of women who have become part of my support system ever since I started my previous career in management consulting. I told her about the meeting, what was shared with me, and what the next steps were. Of course, I used colorful language to describe the interaction, complete with exclamation points and emojis, to drive home how angry (yes, I'm using the word *angry* here) I felt and how ludicrous it was for me to be called into the meeting in the first place. As was commonplace, the reply was "You need to calm down." "You need to remember that you have unique gifts and skills and that this meeting was not about you." I decided to take the rest of the afternoon off and go home to work out and listen to *What the Most Successful People Do Before Breakfast* by Laura Vanderkam, to clear my head. It took several hours to calm myself.

Later that day, my husband and I were having our regular date night, which consisted of snuggling up together in our media room, catching up on *The Good Doctor*, one of our favorite shows on television. I remember sitting there thinking about everything that had transpired over the last two and a half months, from the meetings that I was cut out of, the backbiting in the office, to today's meeting about receiving a national award. I could feel myself not being able to focus and be present with my husband. He could sense my negative energy, and he was very well aware of the dynamics in the office. He was very supportive of me during that time. This experience took me back to other times in my career and my personal life when I felt bullied by others and how I made myself even smaller by not sticking up for myself, my values, and my brand. It was at that moment that I decided to take action. I thought of the senior leaders in my network who had served as silent sponsors for me, those who were making moves for me and putting me into different opportunities behind the scenes. I also thought about the sponsors that were vocal—the ones who were willing to advocate on my behalf. One name rose to the top, and I will be forever grateful for the phone conversation that ensued.

I walked downstairs into my bedroom to grab my cell phone and sent her a text. I simply said, "I need your advice." She responded within an hour and asked if we could talk over the phone. The conversation we had started as a simple mentoring session on how to navigate this difficult situation. By the time the phone call ended, I felt raw, since I had been candid about being bullied over the past several months. My sponsor was not only appalled by my experience, but she was also willing to take action. I expressed my interest in moving to a different department where I would have the opportunity to thrive and own my work. Over the next two weeks, not only did I move out from under the reporting structure of that former boss, but I was also put into a highly visible role within my organization. Seven months later, I got promoted to my first VP-level position as a result of that work, and I had received even more national accolades, including Modern Healthcare's Top 25 Emerging Leaders, and the beginnings of this passion around sponsorship for women of color was born.

MOVING FROM ANGER TO ADVOCACY

There is nothing worse than having your emotions weaponized against you. We have all heard the language used to describe the women of color in the workplace—everything from the Angry Black Woman to the Quiet Asian Woman, and yet none of those adjectives truly describe who we are as individuals. One of my favorite sponsors, a senior executive in healthcare strategy, always says labels are for jars, and I believe that to be true. To be able to move forward and increase diversity and inclusion at the senior levels of an organization, we have to first start by shutting down these labels and truly investing our time, talent, and resources into helping individual women of color succeed. But really, women of color have a reason to be angry.

Let's take an example from the healthcare industry. While progress has been made globally to increase diversity within healthcare leadership, opportunities continue to exist for the advancement of women of color. According to a 2018 study by the American Hospital Association's Institute for Diversity, only 14 percent of hospital board members and 9 percent of CEOs are minorities.[1] Similarly across all industries, McKinsey and the Leanin.org's 2019 "Women in the Workplace" study found that Black women and women with disabilities face more barriers to advancement, get less support from managers, and receive less sponsorship than other groups of women.[2]

Given these challenges, incremental improvements in diversity through traditional means of coaching, mentoring, and development programs may not be enough to take the bold leaps required to increase percentages of diversity in leadership.

So yes, women of color are angry. We are angry because progress has yet to be made to bring equity into the C-Suite. We are angry because the discourse around diversity and inclusion remains unmatched with action. We are angry because we have every right to be emotional and prioritize diversity as a fundamental cultural right. And now, we know how important advocacy and sponsorship are to change these narratives as we move forward.

2

A RECKONING IS HERE

January 11, 2021, was a particularly memorable day for me, as it signified the beginning of a new reckoning for women in corporate America. It was five days after the deadly insurrection on our nation's capital. I was still trying to digest what happened to democracy in my beloved country through constant news cycles, group texts with friends and family, and reading about the aftermath on social media. That morning, I was getting ready for another day working from home, which in fact was almost a year after I packed up what I could from my office on March 15, 2020. Like many of you reading this book, I headed home thinking that I would only be working remotely for two weeks. How wrong we were, in hindsight. I did what I normally did over the past year. I got up, took a shower, made some tea and a little bit of breakfast and walked twenty paces into my home office. A few hours later, I got a push notification on my iPhone. It was a news update from CNN on the state of our labor economy. The headline read "All of the Jobs Lost in December Were from Women."[1] I had to look at my phone twice just to make sure that I read the headline correctly. I couldn't believe it. One hundred percent of the jobs lost in one month were from women? Up to this point, our news cycle was filled with a very concerning increase in COVID-19 deaths and the impact that the pandemic had on the global workforce. Several of my friends and colleagues from other health systems had been laid off or furloughed—many of them women. I rubbed my eyes quickly and picked up my phone to open the article and read it more thoroughly. Yes, it was true. The vast majority of jobs, 140,000 of them, lost in December 2020 were from women. I gasped and quickly texted the article to several of my closest girlfriends. My phone was buzzing every three seconds with text replies. "I can't believe it!" one of my coworkers said. Another sent a series of crying emojis. One of the women in my networking group who had left the workforce to take care of small children at home during the pandemic simply texted back, "This is a shit show." I went back to the article to read it again. Not only were the statistics so alarming for women in general, but they were also particularly devastating for women of color. COVID-19 has had an exponential impact on communities of color and specifically Black and Brown women adversely impacted by the job market and the economy. The first thought that popped into my head after getting over my initial rage from this news was, "How are we going to support women when we return to the office?" How are we going to continue the forward momentum over the last decade by helping women achieve their career ambitions and goals? And most importantly, how do we instill trust in Black, Indigenous, and women of color (BIWOC) that their companies will provide the advocacy and resources needed to succeed? Similar reports from other organizations continued to tell a similar story. The Lily highlighted a report from the World Economic Forum two months later stating that it would take another generation, thirty-six more years, before women would be on equal footing with men.[2] A whole generation?! A generation of progress eliminated in less than one year. Think about the world just two years ago. In 2020, we witnessed the horrific murder of George Floyd, and companies started to publicly advocate for racial equality in the workplace. Only recently in 2021 did the NASDAQ require companies to have at least one woman on their board of directors along with one racial minority and a person that identifies as lesbian, gay, transgender, or queer/questioning (LGBTQ). These have been recent developments for which the pandemic may set progress back. It was like a gut punch for women like me who have been championing the advancement of women of color in the workplace. Connections on my LinkedIn feed have shared this article thousands of times within the last hour. The sentiment was the same. We have a lot more work to do and not a whole lot of time left to do it.

Compounding this news was the fact that it would be difficult to encourage women to return to the workforce. The imbalance of power in the family home was evident. Although both men and women were now working almost exclusively from home, the responsibilities of child, elder, and healthcare almost unanimously fell on the shoulders of women. It felt like we collectively jumped into a DeLorean and traveled back fifty years to when these gender dynamics where commonplace. Women began to feel completely overwhelmed, and if you were a single mother, the effects of the pandemic and growing responsibilities in the home made the situation that much worse. People talked about the dual pandemics, COVID-19 and the fight against racial injustice. I offer to you that it was a triple pandemic—with the pandemic of losing women in the workforce. I could feel my frustration and anger boiling inside. It was a mutual feeling that I shared with leaders in my organization and across my industry. This reinforced to me that the work ahead should evolve beyond dialogue. While conversations help us deal with the emotions of this shared experience, it won't change the outcome unless we take action to change the narrative. Actions lead to results.

WHAT THE DATA TELLS US

There is no shortage of think tanks, research associations, and consulting firms that have dug into the data to understand the trends of what has happened to women since the beginning of the pandemic. Like many women executives, I read the "Women in the Workplace" study, published jointly by McKinsey and LeanIn.org every year. For leadership geeks like myself who craved data and insights, this report shows what progress has been made in gender equity and where there continued to be opportunities to make change. The 2021 study, published in September of that year, confirmed my suspicions and yet was still shocking to me. I freely admit that I always jump to the section that talks about women of color because I am desperately hoping for better results. The article talked about the growing burnout for women in executive roles, but a section of the report leapt off the page for me. The name of the section was "Women of Color Lose Ground at Every Step." From entry-level roles to the C-Suite, representation by women of color dwindles from 17 percent to a dismal 4 percent.[3] No doubt, this number worsened as a result of attrition in the labor force due to COVID-19. An alarming trend highlighted by the report is that while women of color continue to experience micro aggressions at work, active allyship by white counterparts is going down. We'll define these commonly used terms of mentorship, allyship, and sponsorship later in the book. The perception that white colleagues have about their allyship is also vastly different from what women of color deemed to be meaningful support. For example, the study asked respondents which allyship actions are the most meaningful, and there was a stark contrast between white women and women of color. Sixteen percent of white women felt that mentoring and sponsoring women of color is meaningful versus 25 percent of women of color.[4] Additionally, advocating for new opportunities for women of color also had a large gap, with 30 percent of white women believing this to be meaningful versus 44 percent of Black women.[5] This misalignment between understanding what is meaningful to support women of color in the workplace will undoubtedly cause problems as we return to the office.

Tennis legend Billie Jean King funded her own survey of women of color in the workplace in November 2021 as well.[6] In her study, *PowHer Redefined: Women of Color Reimagining the Workplace*, twelve hundred women of color were surveyed, including Asian, Latinx, Black, Native, and mixed-race professionals. The results were equally troubling. Sixty-six percent of respondents said that they didn't have a sponsor in the workplace, and 75 percent felt that they needed to prove themselves over and over again just to feel valued by their colleagues.[7] As a Black woman, I can relate to and accept these findings as I have personally experienced these feelings at various points in my career. In October 2021, I spoke to a group of female physicians at Kaiser Permanente on the topic of sponsorship. One of the polling questions asked the audience how many participants have a sponsor? Out of the twenty-three attendees, only 6 percent said that they had a sponsor that was championing their career. I asked the same question on a webinar with the Healthcare Businesswomen's Association, and the results were similar. Only 31 percent of attendees said that they had a sponsor, and more shockingly, more than 60 percent said they didn't even know if they had a sponsor.

The research becomes even more alarming when we look at pay inequities for women of color across all industries. Whether it's higher education, financial services, retail, or hospitality, BIPOC women earn significantly less than their white female counterparts or their white male counterparts. Black women, multiracial Black women, and Hispanic women earn anywhere from $0.57 to $0.64 to the dollar, compared with white, non-Hispanic women ($0.79) and white, non-Hispanic men ($1.00).[8] This further exacerbates the challenges that women of color face every day at work. Working harder for less pay supports the notion that women of color continue to be undervalued for their gifts and abilities. Payscale took this research one step further and examined the intersectionality of sponsorship by race and ethnicity with the future earning power of the protégé. In its groundbreaking report, Payscale concluded that women of color who are sponsored by white males have a higher earning potential overall than women of color that are sponsored by other women of color.[9] Not only do women of color receive less allyship and sponsorship, but we also have to be strategic on who sponsors us to ensure we receive the economic benefits of sponsorship. In essence, our earning potential is in part in the hands of our sponsors.

Let's not forget the impact that COVID-19 has had on highlighting its gross disparities in care for women of color. The coronavirus wreaked havoc on many communities and especially communities of color. There were higher infection rates for Black and Latina women, and there was a lack of sufficient access to testing early on in the pandemic. Additionally, the majority of essential workers, employees that were required to provide support on the frontlines, were women.[10] Hospitalization and death rates have also been considerably higher for people of color and especially women of color over the last two years. Individual mental wellness has taken a backseat to more pressing healthcare issues for the broader family, particularly in households of color.

This data should come as a shock to no one, especially if you are a corporate leader. There is an abundance of studies that support the business case on investing and providing women of color with robust sponsorship opportunities to improve the pipeline of leadership. The question becomes, "What actions will we take to create these opportunities"?

RACE AND BELONGING IN THE NEW NORMAL WORKPLACE

Heading into the fall of 2021, several media outles suggested a massive return to the office. At the time, mask mandates were being lifted across the United States and in many other countries. Vaccines were being rolled out at various paces, but there was a collective hope that there was a light at the end of this pandemic tunnel. Major corporations were even setting dates for the return and trying to figure out how to manage social distancing while creating a sense of comfort and calm for employees concerned about in-person events. There was energy and momentum along with excitement about the prospect of being able to connect with colleagues without Zoom, Microsoft Teams, or other platforms. However, there was an undercurrent of anxiety about the return. I had an informal conversation with a friend of mine who worked in financial services. She is a Latina and was skeptical about moving to a fully remote work environment because she felt that as she wasn't visible in the office she would be overlooked. Over an eighteen-month period, she grew to really enjoy working virtually. It allowed her to spend more time with her kids and even create space for her to take up more hobbies since she didn't have a commute every day. When we spoke about what it would feel like to return to the daily grind of being in the office, she was worried. Honestly, I was shocked. This should have been exactly what she wanted, more visibility in the office so that her leadership would remember her name and feel a connection to her. Surprisingly, she told me she felt relieved working from home because she wouldn't have the same experience with micro aggressions and dealing with the largely homogeneous leadership team that she worked for. She had greater psychological safety from the comfort of her home than she did when she was physically in the office.

She is not alone in this sentiment. Women of color felt uncomfortable in the physical workplace before the pandemic, and working remotely brought a sense of peace. As employees were encouraged or mandated to return to the office, women of color were reluctant to do so. What type of environment would welcome us back? How do we manage the mental trauma of not only being physically back in the office but then having to work even harder to gain the visibility and have the achievements that would position us for success? Future Forum, a research group that focuses on workplace issues, also examined this phenomenon by surveying ten thousand workers on the topic of remote work. One of the findings from the survey was that Black workers are happier in their jobs when they work remotely.[11] Part of the reason for this satisfaction is that workers of color feel that they can be their authentic selves when they are at home instead of the office. There is no code-switching involved, a practice that many people of color use to fit in with predominantly white cultures.

A RECIPE FOR A RECKONING

Let's put this all together. Women have lost considerable ground in the last eighteen to twenty-four months in the workforce and have lost jobs at an unprecedented rate. Women of color have been adversely impacted by COVID-19 due to issues with health equity, current experiences in the physical workspace, and bearing the brunt of taking on more responsibilities in the home environment. It becomes even more important for executives, leaders, and managers to understand how sponsorship can help create a welcoming environment when women of color return to the workplace. It is also crucial to ensure that women of color do not lose ground in their career advancement due to the impacts of COVID-19 and the conflicts that arise in taking care of family and prioritizing personal well-being. If not, this workplace reckoning will continue to see large numbers of

Black and Brown women voluntarily leaving the workplace or opting to slow the pace of their career progression because it is too challenging to manage all of the stressors associated with managing daily life.

MY PERSONAL ACCOUNTABILITY

Eight months before the pandemic, I published an article in *Forbes*. It was a declaration of my commitment to sponsor one hundred women of color in healthcare. At the time, I thought about the impact that I wanted to make over the next ten years to help women of color in the workplace, as I had grown weary of the lack of progress. Women of color were still grossly underrepresented in positions of leadership and power. I figured that sharing my goals in this regard would inspire other leaders, like me, to become more fervent advocates for diversity and inclusion. Roughly a month before my company moved to remote work, I received a ping on Twitter from someone who had read my *Forbes* article, which had been tweeted earlier that day. I was unsure when *Forbes* would publish the article, and I had not yet received a notification of the publication time. I clicked on the link that was sent to me, and my article titled "Why I'm Sponsoring 100 Women of Color in Healthcare by 2030" was staring me in the face. The tweets and retweets started pouring in. I was elated that my article about sponsorship made it into one of the most influential publications that millions of people read daily for news on business and leadership. It was a commitment that I truly believed in and also one that I felt would inspire other leaders.

I had no idea that less than a month later, we would be dealing with the deadliest pandemic of our time. I felt a bit hopeless, as I knew that the pandemic would be the beginning of a ripple effect that would have dire consequences for the workforce. The impact of COVID-19 transcended issues of public health. It impacted the global economy and everyone's concept of what *normal* was. Originally, launching my initiative and sparking conversation about sponsorship was supposed to happen in normal times—whatever this means to us now. Little did I know how critical the concept of sponsorship would be, given our new normal. Even before the pandemic, there was a need for greater dialogue about how to advance women of color in their careers. The pandemic shined a light on the lack of diverse representation in leadership as more and more women decided to leave the workforce. Managing fulltime jobs, kids, sick family members all became too great of a task for any individual to handle. Many women also made decisions to protect their mental wellness by leaving the workforce altogether, which has created an uphill battle for the return to work. And when women "return to work," what environment will they be returning to? Will their organization continue to allow flexibility and where they choose to work? Have companies evolved and matured to accept alternatives and options to working in person? These were all questions that needed to be answered, and the answers needed to come from executive leaders instead of the employees that have been impacted.

HOW WE MOVE FORWARD TOGETHER

I have thought about this question a lot over the past year: How do we move forward together? The reality is that there is work to be done for both women of color professionals with career goals to achieve and to organizations that have committed to advancing diversity, equity, and inclusion in the workplace. If you are a business leader reading this book, I have a message for you. One fundamental belief we should vow to share is that we must shed the common storylines and misconceptions about why corporations are lacking diversity in leadership. You have to be willing to open your eyes and see yourself, as an executive and leader, as a core variable in the equation. We cannot rest on the assumption that women of color are not doing the work. We cannot rest on the assumption that women of color would have all the tools and resources to be successful if they simply "worked harder." Yes, this is something that I have been told in my career by a previous boss. We must be willing to point the finger at ourselves and critically evaluate how we have shown up to support Black, Asian, Latina, and Native women in our environments. The first question we should be asking our-selves regularly is, "How many Black and Brown women are in my professional orbit?" I'm not talking simply about acquaintances or someone you have casually met. How many women of color do you engage with on a daily basis? How well to you understand their lived experience in your workplace? Have you genuinely connected with a woman of color in the past six to twelve months? These are the critical questions that put you on the path to demonstrating your commitment to diversity and inclusion. Once you have completed this self-assessment, it is time to take action. This book will provide you with examples of how you can do so.

Additionally, if you are a woman of color looking for sponsor-ship, don't work harder. Work more *strategically*. You've done the work, and now it is time to think about what you want to achieve in your career. Where do you want your career to go? What specific actions would you like a sponsor to take on your behalf to help you get there? Are there executives in your network today with whom you have relationships that can help you? If not, how can you be in-tentional about developing those relationships in the next year? Use the insights from this book as a way to reframe things like networking and mentoring to take your career development to the next level.

Last, we collectively need to need to say this together. Lack of diversity in leadership is not a pipeline issue. It is a sponsorship issue.

3

IT'S NOT A PIPELINE ISSUE

December 10, 2019, started off on the wrong foot. I slept through my alarm, which means that I missed my morning workout and meditation. To inspire me to shake it off and start anew, I looked in my gratitude journal to reflect on what I had been grateful for the previous week. Apparently, six days ago, I had written only one word. I was grateful for "kindness." I actually remembered why I wrote that word on that specific day. I was completing my daily commute to work and decided to stop by my local Starbucks for my standard coffee order: a tall Blonde Vanilla Latte, extra hot. I proceeded to the drive-through, made it to the order window, and the barista said to me, "The person in front of you already paid for your order." I was completely in shock for the moment, and then offered to pay for the order for the person behind me. It was clear that the person behind me was ordering for employees at their office because the order came to a whopping $24.11. However, I gladly paid for the order, put on one of my favorite podcasts from the Ellevate Network, and drove the twenty-five minutes it takes to get to the office. That act of kindness stuck with me all day and I found myself doing other random acts of kindness because it actually felt really good. I reflected on the concept of kindness over the subsequent days and how I have been extended kindness in my career.

This experience at Starbucks took me back to August 2018, when I was at my lowest point at work. I was in the thick of being bullied by a former boss and trying to figure out a way to protect my personal and professional brand within my network. On one of my commutes home, a former colleague of mine gave me a call as a way to cheer me up and to remind me that this too shall pass. She reinforced the great work I had done on the team and how she felt that I was serving as an inspiration to other Black women. She encouraged me to give one of my sponsors a call simply to ask for advice on how I should navigate this challenging situation of having a leader using their power and influence in hopes of getting me fired from my job. I did as she coached me to do, and within two weeks of that conversation I had a new high-visibility role within my organization and a renewed outlook on what it means to advocate for yourself. It was her kindness and the kindness of several sponsors that enabled me to claw my way out of darkness and despair and into a very bright future where I could thrive. I continued to wonder how many other Black women have experienced something similar yet had no advocates and no outlets. These thoughts continued to stay with me for the months and years to come.

So back to the day in question. December 10, 2019, was a particularly special day because it was the first time I had discussed with a colleague the need to be intentional about advocating for women of color in the workplace. As I mentioned before, I was already starting my day later than anticipated, and I was rushing to get ready for work. I had just taken my dog, Agnes, out for her morning walk and threw my laptop, keys, and notebook into my work bag. I sometimes reserve my commute time to connect with colleagues, and this morning, I was connecting with a senior leader at work who was also an advocate for me. She had been at our organization for over twenty years and is not only well respected, but has amassed a devoted following of associates because of her leadership style and courage to voice her opinions about the next generation of leaders. I was sharing with her how excited I was that our organization was starting an employee resource group (ERG) for African American and Black women and how honored I was to be leading one of the committees on mentorship and sponsorship. As we were discussing our mutual excitement, this particular senior leader admitted something that literally took all of the air out of my lungs. She said with a serious tone, "I have to admit, I don't know which Black women are in our pipeline for the next promotions." On the one hand, she was approaching our discussion with humility by making this admission. On the other, I felt a sense of rage. How is it that we don't know the names of Black women that are high performers with high potential in our organization and are ready for an executive promotion? She paused for a few seconds and then asked me, "Would you be willing to provide some names? I'd like to make a list and start working this up the chain." My initial reaction internally was "You've got to be fucking kidding me!" Why on earth would I need to come up with a list? This leader had the positional power and greater visibility across the organization to easily, in my mind, write down ten names of Black and Brown women she has engaged with who could be the start of this "pipeline" list. I took a few breaths and told her that I would think about it and get back to her in the next few days. While I knew this leader was coming from a good and noble place, it reinforced for me that organizations like mine have not prioritized the need to advance women of color with intentionality.

Later that evening, I was sitting at home thinking about our conversation, the lack of a pipeline for women of color, and also this concept of kindness. I thought deeply about being asked to put together a list, but most importantly, that I too had power and influence within my organization. If there was anyone that had a passion around advocating for women of color in the workplace, it would be me. While I thought putting together a list of high-potential women of color would be a great start, I knew that I could do better than that. In fact, I wasn't even sure what would happen with this list. Will it go into a Black hole with human resources (HR)? Will the women that I placed on this list find out and be upset? What about other women that I know are high potential that might inadvertently get left off of this list? What happens then? So many questions swirled in my mind to the point of me abandoning the idea of putting together a list altogether. Instead, I thought more directly about setting a goal for myself.

I believe that in order for others to advocate for you, you have to be willing to advocate for others. I have been blessed to have advocates in my network who mobilized to help me continue down my path. Through building my network both internally and externally from my organization, I have met hundreds of Black and Brown women that are doing amazing things within my industry. And in almost all cases, these women would benefit from an additional boost of advocacy where they could have a larger platform and greater visibility to continue becoming the powerhouse women they were meant to be. I also wanted to take this moment to inspire my fellow colleagues to pay it forward. The senior leader that wanted to create a pipeline list could easily begin sponsoring these women and use her capital—political and social—to do so.

I thought the first place to start for me was to share my story of sponsorship. I put pen to paper and wrote an article for *Forbes* about my experience being sponsored and how it transformed my career. In this article, I went one step further and committed to sponsoring one hundred women of color in healthcare by 2030. This wasn't simply a commitment. It was also a way for me to hold myself accountable to helping Black women like me succeed. I thought if I could sponsor one hundred women, then other executives like me could do the same. This commitment would also move representation in senior leadership from dialogue to action. We could create an abundance of lists of names of high-potential Black women, or we could simply sponsor these women and develop them for the future. I am betting on sponsorship as the key mechanism to increase representation for the future of leadership.

The pipeline already exists. We just have to be willing to amplify the pipeline through sponsorship.

WHAT IS THE PIPELINE?

The first time I had heard of the concept of a pipeline was when I worked in management consulting for Deloitte Consulting, one of the Big Four consulting firms. Senior partners would talk about rising talent in terms of which employees had the skills, knowledge, and abilities to be ready for the next-level promotion. It was fascinating listening to who was identified as being "ready" for that next step.

What differentiated the skillsets of employees deemed "ready" from those of employees who were not ready?

Many organizations spend a fortune on recruiting diverse talent. It is estimated that diversity and inclusion is an eight-billion-dollar business. Several organizations are recognized for their recruiting efforts through awards for being top companies for multicultural women, Black women, and other groups as a competitive advantage.

Additionally, many companies tout their recruitment process and their selection process as being very selective. They claim they have a high bar that candidates need to meet in order to be hired and if selected, they have surpassed that bar. I remember receiving my offer letter to join Deloitte Consulting, which is commonly cited as one of the most selective management consulting firms in the world and is said to be as selective as Harvard when recruiting new talent to join their ranks. Knowing that I had met these high standards made me feel exceptionally proud. I was also excited to know that I would be supported in my career development going forward. Many applicants feel this way after going through rounds and rounds of interviews, refreshing their résumés, and getting their offer. So we have talent coming through our front doors who meet or exceed the requirements for hire. The question then becomes, Why do we continue to have issues with creating a pipeline of talent, or a list of associates ready for promotion?

THE SEDUCTION

When I speak to my protégés and mentees about their experience in corporate America, many have shared that they feel as if they are alone, in a kayak, trying to navigate difficult waters. They are left to advocate for their continued advancement by themselves. Recruitment can feel, in a lot of ways, like a seduction. You are wined and dined, given the pitch for the organization, told about all of its efforts around diversity. Once you join, you realize that there are many more challenges that you will face. You've done your research.

You've seen the company selected as the best place to work for minorities, and then you take a look at their leadership team and realize that you don't see yourself or anyone like you in those ranks. You may see a couple of leaders of color at the executive levels, but the path to getting there is nebulous.

Most recently, I spoke with one of my mentees about her job search and the excitement she had about being selected for a new role at a well-known, national, for-profit healthcare system. She only stayed at that organization for one month. During our conversation, she shared how the recruitment team targeted her pretty aggressively based on her background and the fact that she was a diverse candidate. The organization had a prominent reputation for supporting diverse talented people and helping them grow in their careers. In her first week on the job, she realized that not only was the culture not right for her but also that the actual support for Black women in the organization was lacking. I asked her what she meant by support because I am a very tactical person at heart. First and foremost, there were very few women of color in executive leadership at her organization. It was difficult for her to picture herself getting promoted to an executive role because she would be the only one that looked like her in leadership. In her discussions with her direct supervisor, she shared her concerns about how she felt—being one of only a few Black women in similar roles. There was very little empathy on the part of her boss. In fact, he shared that a person's success was based upon their individual contributions and that she should focus on doing excellent work—a common trope that many Black women are told is necessary to get ahead. She also experienced frequent micro aggressions including colleagues commenting about her natural hair style as well as discussion about her educational background not being standard (she graduated from a historically Black college [HBCU]) for someone in her role. She felt that she was being continually micromanaged and that every misspelling or grammatical error was being looked at under the strongest microscope one could find. In one instance, she was having a discussion with a colleague about musical preferences and discussed how she was a big fan of the Foo Fighters. A colleague looked at her with immense surprise and said, "I didn't know people like you listened to that kind of music." Needless to say, she resigned after only twenty-one days in that new position, having uprooted herself and her family to take on a leadership role in a new market.

RETAINING TALENT

The picture is much grimmer when you look at the development of diverse talent from a retention perspective. It is estimated that employee attrition rates among Black, Brown, and other underrepresented groups are two times higher than those of non-diverse talent. Those millions of dollars that organizations have invested in trying to solve the problem of lack of diversity end up producing few results. It is common for organizations to enact programs like formal mentoring and system resource groups designed to help engage diverse talent in their career development and keep them in the company. It is all too prevalent to try to solve the issue of retention by assigning rising diverse talent to mentors who would serve as a resource for advice on navigating office politics, developing themselves in a career, or being a sounding board to their career plans. However, advancement to the next level of your career continues to stagnate even when giving a mentor to help you think through how to position yourself for that next step. Because a good mentor is not enough.

One day I sat down with a senior leader at my former organization and invited her out for coffee. I wanted to better understand how she got to her level and the specific steps she took to put her on that path to success. I will never forget what she said to me. She mentioned a professional working relationship she developed with a senior white male partner who noticed her potential early in her career and continued to advocate for her for promotions at each level over the past five years. She was one of the few Black leaders that made it to partner in such a short period. She said that his advocacy via speaking with his fellow partners about who should be promoted was increasingly valuable; and that advocacy relationship continued even after she made it to partner. She told me that without that advocacy, she would have either left the firm or been left to wade in the water for years before realizing that she would never get the support needed to advance.

THE FAILURE RATE OF RETENTION

That conversation stuck with me as I continued down my path. I wondered how many other talented diverse professionals were given that same advice—to seek a sponsor intently and unapologetically. If you do a quick Google search on strategies for career advancement, you will see an abundance of hits related to mentorship and how important mentorship is in crafting yourself as a leader and as a professional. Over the past several months, I've been going on a listening tour with colleagues both within and outside my organizations just to test the waters on their perspective on retaining diverse talent. What was surprising about those conversations was how many Black female leaders believed that if they kept their heads down and did great work, they would be promoted and given opportunities. These women were at the early stages of their executive careers. They talked about mentorship and the importance of finding mentors. They even discussed experiences that they'd had with mentors and the advice that they received that was helpful for them to develop their career plans and their networking plans. But even with all of the mentoring programs they participated in, they still felt that there was a glass ceiling in their organizations.

WHY DIVERSE TALENT IS LEAVING

Over the past seventeen years in my professional career, I've often thought about why I decided to make the transitions I did. Some of the time it was for better work-life harmony. As I progressed in my career and became more senior, I realized the value of working for an organization where I felt supported and where I could be myself. I believe that many Black and Brown professionals struggle with the desire to succeed in their careers and to work for a company that values their authenticity—providing them the freedom and space to be their authentic selves. I have seen an increase in the number of Black women who have decided to leave corporate America and start their own businesses. They felt that they couldn't have the impact that they wanted within the four walls of the organizations they had belonged to. Being their own bosses allowed them the ability to lead in the most authentic way to themselves but also allowed them to have a direct impact on improving the lives of the people they serve. More and more diverse women, for example, are putting a premium on their happiness and mental wellness and not wanting to fight the uphill battles of institutionalized and systemic racism to reach the level of success they deserve. From 2007 to 2018, women-owned businesses grew by 54 percent, and that number nearly tripled, specifically for Black women, growing by 164 percent.[1]

Data overwhelmingly suggests that the feelings that Black and Brown women have in the workplace are valid. While Black women are the most educated demographic in the United States, in terms of Bachelor and associate degrees, opportunities for advancement and pay equity continue to dwindle.[2] According to the Institute for Women's Policy Research, Black women will not achieve pay equity with white males until the year 2130.[3]

So why are talented, diverse professionals increasingly leaving organizations? One thought is that younger employees in particular expect organizations to match their actions to their words on supporting diversity in senior leadership. A study by Deloitte states that 72 percent of employees are considering leaving their organizations for other companies that put a premium on diversity and inclusion initiatives.[4] Companies must demonstrate their support of diversity by ensuring that diverse talent has the same access to success as their white counterparts. Introducing and exposing Black and Brown talent to senior leadership with intentionality through high-visibility enterprise projects and selecting diverse talent for career-development programs with tangible outcomes are ways to accomplish this. Incoming talent also has a higher level of discernment at looking at the makeup of senior leadership as a demonstration of their commitment to diversity and inclusion. If a company prides itself on being a top organization for diversity and inclusion, and the C-Suite is completely homogenous, new talent will see that as being disingenuous to diversity and inclusion and damaging to the brand.

The other reason why new talent is leaving is the lack of transparency, diversity, and inclusion data. Employees expect that leadership will be open and authentic about the challenges they face with diversifying their leadership rather than treating that data as a Black box. According to *Fortune* magazine and a survey conducted in 2017, only 3.2 percent of the Fortune 500 companies openly shared diversity data based on race and gender.[5] This lack of transparency coupled with the lived experiences of diverse professionals creates an environment of distrust and disillusionment with an employee's ability to succeed at that company. To strengthen the relationship with diverse employees, organizations need to be willing to admit their faults and share not only their baseline data around race and gender but also the progress that the organization is making to increase diversity in leadership.

REFRAMING THE LEAKY "DIVERSITY" PIPELINE

With high levels of attrition at companies across the globe, many organizations are suffering from "leaky pipeline syndrome." The leaky pipeline is the phenomenon that occurs when organizations invest substantial amounts of money to recruit diverse talent only to have that talent leave the organization on progression to a people-manager role because of a perceived and real lack of investment in the employee's career development. Plenty of talent goes into the pipeline—or the talent pool—and starts to seep out once the employee has lived experience at work. Yes, the organization is lauded for its commitment to diversity, and that diversity can be seen in entry-level positions with the company. But as you look up the ladder, the view is very different, and little ethnic and racial diversity exists. Companies are facing a conundrum. In one instance, leadership laments the fact that there isn't a pipeline of diverse talent ready for that next level of leadership. In the second instance, organizations complain that once they get diverse talent into the "pipeline," that same talent seeks greener pastures elsewhere. The fundamental notion of these two instances absolutely must change to foster the right types of relationships with diverse talent and support their growth. On a very basic level, organizations need to believe that they already possess the diverse talent ready for that next level of leadership. If an organization spends thousands of dollars recruiting talent, the organization should ensure that this same talent has received the training, exposure, and development needed to climb the corporate ladder. And if for some reason an organization has failed to provide that education and growth for its diverse talent, it needs to be willing to admit it and unapologetically invest resources in helping future talent succeed.

I've spoken to colleagues of mine across the country that are dealing with this very issue. They are leaders trying to advocate for greater investment in diverse talent through targeted programming on executive presence, stretch assignments, and other ways to elevate the leadership capabilities of their employees. Many times, they are met with rebuttals about the lack of pipelines or the leaky pipeline. Collectively, the consensus is that these challenges need to be reframed so that organizations take responsibility for their role in failing to advance or develop diverse talent within their four walls. When I share my journey at conferences, on podcasts, or in webinars, I commonly talk about how leaders served as sponsors for me in my career journey. That sponsorship has shown measurable success in enabling me to be promoted to manager and executive roles. There have even been times in my career when I felt that I was alone in my growth and development and that I needed to own my career to be successful. But the times when I was able to get promoted or take a leap and be responsible for larger scopes of work were due to several sponsors that had advocated for me with leadership making the decisions on promotions.

This is one of the main reasons why I champion career sponsorship as the mechanism to advance BIPOC individuals to leadership levels. I hope that other executives will internalize their responsibility to sponsor talented professionals who don't look like them and be bold and courageous in their endeavors. Let's not simply talk about the need for diversity and inclusion but take action that will have a long-lasting impact on changing the narrative around diversity and leadership.

DEFINING IMPORTANT TERMS

Before we move on in this book, I think it's important to have common language around several the commonly used terms *allyship, mentorship,* and *sponsorship.* I have seen these words used interchangeably, but the fact is they have very different meanings and purposes. I will provide more tangible examples of sponsorship in future chapters.

Allyship is an essential term when we discuss how to support women of color in the workplace and is the foundation for accelerating diversity within organizations. It occurs when a person of privilege works in partnership with underrepresented groups of people to remove the constructs that challenge or threaten that group's ability to thrive. *Allyship* is a noun, but more importantly, it is a verb. The best allies educate themselves on the issues of marginalized groups and seek to understand how they can behave in a way that demonstrates their support of their needs. Coincidentally, *allyship* was Dictionary .com's 2021 Word of the Year; it has also defined *allyship* as "the role of a person who advocates for inclusion of a marginalized or politicized group in solidarity but not as a member."[6] It is no surprise that *allyship* is used in the context of both mentorship and sponsorship due a common set of principles. All three require empathy and action. The difference here is that not all allies are mentors or sponsors. Mentorship and sponsorship require a set of skills that focus on the development and professional growth of the other person. Allyship is more about creating an atmosphere of belonging in the workplace where people of color feel embraced, seen, and respected because the ally is practicing their empathy. Allyship actions do not have to be grand gestures. Even the smallest of actions have a big impact. Examples of allyship include amplifying the voices of BIPOC employees by ensuring they get credit for their ideas in work meetings or inviting diverse employees to discussions or gatherings where there is opportunity for them to have greater exposure. Additionally, an ally will speak up when witnessing racist or sexist remarks in the workplace or observing discrimination—even when a person of color is not part of the conversation. In fact, mentors and sponsors that embrace diversity begin their journey as allies because allyship is grounded in humility and education. I encourage any executive looking to sponsor diverse talent to consider practicing allyship by reading books on antiracism, particularly those written by people of color. Books such as *So You Want to Talk about Race*, by Ijeoma Oluo, or *Why I'm No Longer Talking to White People about Race*, by Reni Eddo-Lodge, provide viewpoints and perspectives from Black women with lived experiences that will open your eyes to why education on race and gender are critical to becoming an effective ally.

Mentorship is one of the most commonly used terms in professional development. In short, mentorship is the act of providing guidance, direction, and teaching to a less experienced person—a mentee. It is practiced both formally and informally and can have a lasting impact on the mentee's career. I remember my earliest mentors, who have given me pearls of wisdom around leadership that I still practice to this day. Mentors can be senior leaders or associates at the entry level. The focus of mentors is to *advise*, one of the two A's that I use to distinguish mentorship from sponsorship. Examples of mentorship include a manager who helps one of their mentees navigate the unwritten rules of the office or provides feedback on a presentation their mentee made at the last team meeting. Mentors also serve as a sounding board for emotional support if a mentee is facing a challenge at work or in their career. Additionally, there is little expected in return from the mentee, and mentors are generally enthused and honored to provide advice to someone who deems their guidance worthy. One of the reasons I believe that mentorship sometimes gets equated to sponsorship is that there is an underlying assumption that mentors are also sponsors. There is a common belief that if someone is willing to mentor you, naturally they will also be a vocal and active sponsor for you. While this can sometimes be true, it is not always true because of the difference in perceived or apparent risk in sponsorship. There are also times in your career when having a mentor makes more sense. I have always embraced mentorship, even as a senior leader, but it had more of an impact in the early years of my career when I didn't understand workplace dynamics. I needed guidance on my ability to communicate, how to dress professionally, or even how to be an effective manager. My mentors taught and pushed me to be better, and their payback was seeing me succeed while mentoring others. Sponsorship, on the other hand, ups the ante.

Sponsorship, in my opinion, is the highest form of support for women of color in the workplace. It is the second of the two "A's"— sponsors are *advocates*. Sponsors take an active and special interest in developing a person's career—namely a protégé's. They put their skin in the game by going one step further from mentorship and put their brand, reputation, and influence on the line to create space for you to succeed. Whether this is in approaching their boss to get approval for your promotion or appointing you to an influential committee at work, they are your brand ambassadors. If a colleague asks them who is on their short list of high potential leaders, your name is at the top, and they say your name unapologetically and without pause. We have seen this play out on the national stage. President Joe Biden's endorsement of Kamala Harris helped to create history in the United States when she was elected as our first female, Black, and South Asian vice president. Typically, sponsors are senior-level executives, due to their political capital and deep-reaching influence, are well networked, and are risk takers themselves. The sponsors with the most impact have benefited from sponsorship over their careers, so they intimately understand how to sponsor effectively and why it is critical for career growth. One of the key differences between sponsorship and mentorship is that in sponsorship, a lot is expected in return from the protégé. If the protégé somehow fails to live up to the sponsor's expectations or even their act of sponsorship, it could be detrimental to the sponsor's brand. This drives home the point about the risks that many executives believe exist with sponsorship and could be the reason why some are reluctant to become active sponsors themselves. With mentorship, if a mentee decides not to take their mentor's advice or perhaps the advice wasn't helpful, the mentor is largely unaffected. Even in these cases, the mentee is still thankful for the coaching and time that the mentor provided to them. In sponsorship, if a protégé fails to live up to the promotion they received, the sponsor could be put in the hot seat for their advocacy if the person was not ready for that opportunity. Sponsors want assurance that their support for you will not only benefit your success but also theirs as well.

With these foundational definitions of *allyship*, *mentorship*, and *sponsorship*, let's delve further into sponsorship and what this looks and feels like for women of color professionals.

4

SPONSORSHIP LOOKS DIFFERENT FOR WOMEN OF COLOR

After five fulfilling years working at one of the largest health systems in the Southeast, I decided it was time for me to pivot in my career on February 25, 2021. Although I loved healthcare strategy and corporate development, my soul had been pulling me in a different direction. My passion for advocacy and sponsorship along with my gravitation toward the people side of the busines had me explore other opportunities during 2020. I wanted a career that would allow me to marry this passion with having tangible impact on placing underrepresented minorities in senior-level roles across industries. I found myself pivoting back to consulting, talent consulting to be exact. I accepted a position with Egon Zehnder, the world's leading talent advisory firm, and it was the perfect next chapter for me to pursue these passions. Leaving Atrium Health was certainly bittersweet. But I knew that the only way for me to move forward in finding great, diverse leadership was to practice what I preach in my profession.

I made a bold decision to not rush into starting my next role. After getting my second shot of the Pfizer vaccine to protect against Covid-19, I immediately took two whole weeks off. This was the first time in my career history that I actually took time off in between jobs. Usually, if I left my previous job on a Friday, I'd be right back to work on Monday. This time would be different. I wanted time for myself to do, honestly, whatever I wanted to do. I do admit that after only two days of my vacation I had started to feel restless and bored, but I always reminded myself how blessed I was to have this time, and it jolted me right back into enjoying the rest and relaxation. For me, this included napping, catching up with friends that I had lost touch with during the pandemic, reading, and of course indulging in all of my guilty pleasures—namely watching any shows that Netflix recommended. It was blissful and liberating. I frequently questioned why I had never done this before, but then I remembered how conditioned I had been by negative mentors throughout my career to look at taking vacation or time off as a negative quality in a leader. I am so glad that my thinking has evolved over the past few years, and I embrace "unplugging" from work as part of my mental wellness—a key part in being sponsor-ready, in my opinion.

During this time off, I was still waiting to hear back from my literary agent, Tamar Rydzinski, about whether my book proposal would get picked up. Today, after several agonizing months, I heard from her that I had scored my first book deal. I remember clicking on the email, reading the first few sentences, and squeaking so loudly that my husband upstairs heard me. I was elated, yet immediately scared. Yes, sponsorship is a topic that I think the world needs to hear more about, but I was still unsure about how my message would land—especially, one of the key messages that I think is the ugly truth about sponsorship for diverse women in the workplace. The ugly truth is that sponsorship is truly lacking for BIPOC women across all professional industries. Mentorship, while absolutely necessary for women of color, is a mainstream concept. It's sponsorship that will drive a change in leadership behavior toward elevating Black and Brown women to executive roles. It's sponsorship that is the engine for finding diverse talent rather than someone simply stating that diverse talent doesn't exist.

If sponsoring is such a positive behavior to exemplify, why aren't more managers and leaders doing it for their diverse workforce? The answers, I found, were both simple and complicated. Sometimes straightforward, mostly infuriating. And while there are studies that have gone deeper into providing insights into leadership behavior on this topic, we aren't seeing the change in leadership behavior happening fast enough to make dramatic impact on the professional careers of women of color in the next few years.

FEAR AS A DETERRENT OF
INCLUSIVE SPONSORSHIP

I have always believed that fear is a powerful, yet toxic, motivator for personal behavioral change. It makes us uncomfortable, and it forces us to gravitate toward or seek out things that are familiar to us. Fundamentally, I think fear prevents leaders from stepping outside their comfort zones. In doing so, leaders surround themselves with people similar to them, reducing opportunities to broaden their networking circles and perspectives on people that are different from them. Stephanie Bradley Smith is vice president and chief human resources officer for DePaul University and an adjunct faculty member in the Driehaus College of Business. Her article titled "How a Lack of Sponsorship Keeps Black Women Out of the C-Suite" explored what has traditionally held BIPOC women back from senior executive roles—the elusiveness of sponsorship. Over the course of a year, Stephanie aimed to identify the predictors of sponsorship and protégé success for Black women that were positioned within one to two levels of the CEO or president.[1] She unearthed several trends that I, and others, also experienced. For example, she found that sponsors for Black women tended to advocate for them "behind the scenes" and not so much in public view. We all know the power of advocacy, especially when it is done publicly so that your peers and superiors can observe. Courage can be infectious and inspire others to be advocates themselves. Too often, when there is an opportunity in the moment during a meeting to speak up on behalf of a diverse professional, as a sponsor or not, there is silence. I remember being a junior manager in a very high-profile meeting where the leadership was discussing the next five-year strategy for the organization. One of my former colleagues, let's call him Bill, completely talked over another colleague of mine, let's call her Anne, an Asian American rising female executive. It was painful to watch. Even more painful was the silence of Bill's peers, especially "Ernie" who was seemingly a sponsor for Anne. The tension was palpable. The more junior colleagues in the room were shocked that Ernie didn't speak up on

Anne's behalf. She had an amazing idea that was creative, innovative, and certainly something we could implement, about growing our services in the region. After twenty excruciating minutes, the meeting concluded, and a subset of the group, including Ernie and Anne, debriefed. Immediately, Ernie said to the group. "Don't worry. I'll talk to Bill privately." On the surface, that might seem like the right approach to some. Take these sorts of issues into a private setting, and perhaps Bill will be more receptive. The problem with this is that there is power in advocacy in the moment. Not after the meeting. Not over drinks at your favorite bar six hours from now. But right there when the opportunity surfaces. First of all, it addresses the behavior immediately and publicly, so that all parties understand your position and that it's not acceptable. Second, and in my opinion just as important, is that your peers and team members know that you are an advocate for that person. It's public knowledge. People can share anecdotes about how you stepped into your courage and helped Anne when she needed it most. Courage can be infectious. Too often, behind-the-scenes advocacy breeds more silent sponsors. And while we can all probably agree that all forms of sponsorship (public and private) can be helpful, it makes it very difficult for sponsorship to grow when sponsors themselves cannot see it. They cannot touch it. They don't know what it looks and feels like when it's done behind closed doors. The other part to Stephanie's research that I found compelling was what she calls the "challenge of the formation of white male sponsorship." She calls out white male sponsorship specifically in her research, more than likely because white males typically have the most power and influence in corporate governance and social structures. She discusses how white males may feel discomfort with publicly sponsoring BIPOC women because it may show favoritism on their end, or they might have a fear of making promises they weren't sure they could keep. I admit that I had a chuckle when I read this part of the article. I certainly have never experienced a white male with these same fears when sponsoring other white males. In fact, I've actually heard white male executives vouching for their white male protégés freely and openly—even going so far as to proclaim that he is a rising star or someone we should look up to as up-and-comers ourselves. It's always fascinating how changing the race and gender of the protégé seems to invoke a fear of, well, simply leading as an executive and a sponsor.

There were several additional trends mentioned in the article including Black women being excluded from informal social networks, lack of opportunity to connect with white male colleagues, as well as misrepresentation of the sponsor-protégé relationship. These are all certainly true. Personally, I believe that fear on the part of the sponsor is the leading cause of lack of sponsorship for women of color in the workplace. This fear is also coupled with a lack of self-awareness for sponsors on how they are behaving as sponsors as well as a lack of training and examples on how to sponsor in the most effective way. Instead of stepping into your fear and tapping into your curiosity, executives and managers deflect the responsibility of seeking and retaining sponsors solely onto the protégé. I have spoken to senior men and women about their thoughts on why there is a lack of sponsorship for women of color. In all of my conversations over the past several months, the sentiments around sponsorship were outwardly focused on the protégé:

"She's not sponsor-ready. She hasn't done the work."

"She's never told me that she wanted a sponsor. She has to speak up and ask for what she wants."

"I treat all of my colleagues the same. I don't want to give anyone preferential treatment."

"I simply don't have time to actively sponsor anyone."

These are direct quotes from executives I've spoken with. And I do want to note that the last sentiment, while it may be true for some executives, is extremely problematic—it underscores the fact that there are more employees looking for sponsorship than there are active sponsors. But never once did any of these leaders accept responsibility for not sponsoring more women of color. These sentiments also tend to be pervasive in organizational cultures where there is an emphasis on high employee work performance and not so much on apprenticeship or mentorship. Or at least, apprenticeship and mentorship are also happening behind closed doors and in certain professional, social circles. In these environments, it's not surprising that fear is a motivator for some leaders. If you're a retail leader who doesn't hit your sales goals or metrics for the quarter, you may not receive your bonus, or you may be even out of a job. That fear becomes the adrenaline that jumpstarts your energy to reach your next quota. You feel an accountability to yourself and to the business to achieve growth. And if you're an exceptional leader, you place responsibility on hitting those goals on yourself. Developing diverse talent within your organization should be not be viewed differently. It comes back to accountability—the behavior of executives to play a role in advancing diversity within the workplace by identifying, retaining, and advancing people of color.

LACK OF DATA AND INFORMATION ON INCLUSIVE SPONSORSHIP

Who would have thought there would be such a vacuum of information regarding inclusive sponosrship in business books? First of all, I absolutely admire Sylvia Ann Hewlett, author of several acclaimed books on the topic, including *The Sponsor Effect: How to Be a Better Leader by Investing in Others* and *Forget a Mentor, Find a Sponsor: The New Way to Fast Track Your Career.* Her work has certainly thrust sponsorship into professional dialogue around advancing women in the workplace. But outside of her work and a few other notable books focused on this topic, there isn't a wealth of data or information on sponsorship in general. If you are a rising diverse professional and want to learn more about how sponsorship can impact your career, what you'll find is an eclectic mix of articles, books, blogs, and studies that reinforce issues around sponsorship, but not a ton on how to truly seek this information out successfully, given your unique experiences in the workplace. In fact, you'd find much more information on mentorship, but we know that mentorship is simply the first step. Googling mentorship results in 1.36 billion hits, including a glossary definition from Oxford Languages about what mentorship is. On the other hand, you'll get roughly 4.6 billion hits if you google "sponsorship," but the language and definitions are not as consistent. And most of these are focused on sponsorship related to a company's brand.

You'll only get 156 million hits on Google if you change your search strategy to "career sponsorship," and even then, it's still a hodgepodge of everything from how to gain a career sponsor to how to find a sponsor for a sporting event. And outside of the work of Minda Harts and Jovina Ang, there simply isn't enough data, information, or stories on what career sponsorship looks like for women of color. There needs to be more. More stories from Black and Brown women who have been sponsored that show the powerful impact sponsorship had on them versus when they had no sponsor. More stories on sponsorship relationships and outcomes that have propelled women of color forward into senior leadership. And even more stories from sponsors who have made it their professional purpose to invest in diverse talent through advocacy.

Because there is a ton of information on mentorship, it is no surprise that this is where most professionals and companies start their journeys. Mentorship is the first step to providing access to executive leadership for women of color. Sponsorship amplifies this impact significantly.

WOMEN OF COLOR ARE STEERED TOWARD MENTORSHIP OVER SPONSORSHIP

I'm going to say something slightly controversial here, but please know that it comes truly from a good place in wanting to effect change. I'm also speaking from personal experience. I have sat in panel discussions at national conferences focused on women leaders, and the through line is that women tend to be over-mentored and under-sponsored. It is well documented, and if you are a woman reading this book, you are probably nodding your head. I will go several steps further and say that specifically, women of color are over-steered toward mentorship *over* sponsorship.

There are several reasons that this phenomenon—pushing women of color to mentorship—is happening in corporate America.

First, mentorship as a behavior and a concept is generally more understood and is more accessible to women of color. Most professionals have had a mentor, more so than a sponsor. In a lot of ways, mentorship does help solve some of the immediate issues that women of color face daily. Everything from navigating workplace politics and micro aggressions to executive presence and communication are things that a mentor can help with. Generally speaking, executives enjoy coaching and mentoring others. There's an egalitarian aspect to feeling that you can impart your knowledge to someone struggling with a problem. You feel as though you've arrived, and more than likely you are flattered to be a mentor. Second, mentorship gives women of color a safe space to discuss their experiences for the most part, particularly if their mentor has lived experience and can empathize with his or her diverse protégés. Third, mentorship is very much a low-risk activity for executives. Mentees are over-grateful for their mentor's time, and mentors inherently do not have anything more to give than their advice in the relationship. Serving as a mentor is also highly regarded by organizations, and executives serving as mentors are viewed as the gold standard for leadership. In fact, many executives are rewarded for serving as mentors, either through monetary compensation, greater exposure within senior leadership, or external validation (awards and recognition). Because of this, executives will jump at the chance to be mentors, either internally or externally to their companies, thus contributing to a greater supply of mentors over sponsors. Because of this, mentorship has been practiced and written about far more than sponsorship—making sponsorship more elusive, both in practice and accessibility for women of color.

COFFEE AND "VIRTUAL CONVERSATIONS"— REAL TALK ABOUT SPONSORSHIP AS A BIPOC WOMAN

I would be remiss not to share some of the conversations I've had with BIPOC executives on the topic of sponsorship. Everyone I asked was willing to give me their time to discuss their points of view and what they've learned, and all of these conversations were based on their individual lived experiences as women of color in their profession. I spoke with thirty-one women of color, primarily Black, Asian, and multiracial, who were in various seasons in their career, but mostly at the mid- to senior-level in the retail, media, banking, and healthcare industries. Over the course of our thirty-to-sixty-minute discussions, we laughed and "kee-keed" about our work challenges during the pandemic, mutually shared our passions and skepticism about the current state of sponsorship for women of color, and ultimately agreed to all take action to increase opportunities for women of color as active sponsors. Thankfully, being Zoom fatigued was not a deterrent to participation for these ladies, and I selected a handful of discussions to compare and contrast viewpoints as women of color are not a monolith. Where appropriate, I indicated how the interviewee identified by gender and race and/or anonymized their name and title to bring greater comfort to them in sharing their experiences and views.

Case Study #1: I never asked for sponsorship. It came to me organically.[2]

One of my early conversations was with one of my former colleagues, a vice president at one of the largest and most respected global media companies and a professional acquaintance of mine for the past ten years. During my time in management consulting, I had the opportunity to connect with Jill (anonymized for the purposes of this interview), a high-potential woman of color in the firm's human capital practice. She had just been selected for one of the firm's most prestigious development programs, which included a sponsorship to attend a top-ten MBA program and then return to the organization after matriculation. She is currently working on developing a career sponsorship program at her organization and is a passionate diversity, equity, and inclusion (DEI) advocate. I sat down with Jill to get her take on her viewpoints on sponsorship and how it has impacted her career.

What does sponsorship look like and feel like to you?

I have clearly differentiated from mentorship in that sponsorship is someone who is putting their social and political capital on the line in order to advocate for you. They also provide air cover for different things for someone not necessarily in need of "development" but in need of amplification, access, and advice.

How would you differentiate mentorship and sponsorship in your mind?

It's funny that you've asked me this question about differentiating mentorship and sponsorship because I hear the two terms being conflated a lot, when clearly one has a certain purpose and the other has a different purpose. I feel like mentorship is more about advice and guidance—someone that you can go to that helps you work through a tough situation and trying to help you think through things or weigh options. It could be someone that's probably more senior than you. You can also have peer mentors or even folks that are younger than you that can coach you. For example, I have seen younger professionals mentor more seasoned professionals on things like technology. But to me, sponsorship is very much about power and utilizing that power for the sake of helping others with advancement or access to opportunities that will set you up for success. The intention is a little bit different. You also have the level of personal risk that the sponsor needs to be willing to make, which is above and beyond what a mentor would make. The sponsor relationship is more outward facing—helping you to expand your network and connections. The mentor relationship can feel more inward facing—helping you to navigate your current company dynamics.

How have you experienced both mentorship and sponsorship in your career?

I've had both show up in a lot of different ways. When I was working in management consulting, I was a senior consultant, and I was about to be promoted to manager. There was a project that was super high profile—a previous consulting firm had done poorly, and we were brought in at the last minute to help clean it up. A senior manager advocated for me and approached me about wanting to be the project manager. At the time, I would not have actively said yes because I didn't necessarily feel like I was ready. The senior manager said that she put my name in the ring to lead the project, which was in California. I lived in Atlanta so the partner overseeing the project wouldn't have naturally assumed I could handle the travel or manage the work. But she not only recommended me for the role but pushed for me to be in the role. Even after I joined the project, she helped give me insight into like work with that particular partner because that partner had a very specific style. She gave me the ins and outs of how to work with the partner. She was there to support me if something went wrong. She made sure that I succeeded in that role. This is a more explicit example of sponsorship in action for me. There was another situation where a sponsor helped advocate for me to get out of a project. I got nominated for a development program in the human capital practice for high potential talent right before I left the firm. I was so burnt out and overwhelmed—even though I knew it was an honor to be selected. I just honestly knew I couldn't participate. I remember talking to a senior partner in the healthcare practice that was another sponsor for me. He reached out to me and said, "Hey, I'm here to support you" and scheduled meetings with me on a regular basis to help me not feel as overwhelmed. I shared with him about getting selected for this program but how I was feeling with my workload and that I couldn't dedicate the time that was needed to truly participate in the way that I wanted. He listened and said, "It sounds like you already know the answer," and I agreed that I should decline the opportunity. I went to the partner in charge of the program and politely declined, but it didn't work. I went back to him and shared my experience trying to gracefully decline. He said to me, "Go back to him and you say that *I* told you that you need to drop out." When I did that, the partner didn't push me any further to participate. He put himself out there and basically allowed me to put this burden on him. He gave me the cover that I needed. He knew that his name held weight and that his political capital would be respected among his peers.

What characteristics do you feel make a great sponsor?

I know this is not necessarily a characteristic, but I think white men actually serve as the best sponsors because they have the political capital that they can spend freely and go above and beyond. There's a podcast that I listen to—I listen to so many podcasts—but they were talking about sponsorship and how capital is like a bank. If you are a senior Black woman or Asian woman that is the sponsor, they have a little limited amount of political capital so it can actually be more detrimental or risky for them to give away their capital in comparison to a white man. I also think about what the impact is on the sponsor to advocate for diverse talent. I feel like white men also have more of that inherent trust—that people will trust their perspective a lot more than if a Black woman advocates for another Black woman. Unfortunately, in my experience, there is some mistrust when a person of color advocates for another person of color. People might think that they are only advocating for a person of color because they themselves are a person of color—not because the person is talented. I don't believe that a white man would get the same reaction or pause. I'm sad to say that they seem to have more inherent trust within the organization, and their word can be taken at face value. This is how it sometimes plays out. The other thing is most men don't even call it sponsorship. It's simply how they operate—how they advance talented people. It is that thing that they already do for their friends or the guy they played golf with or a college classmate. You have to put a name to it when you talked to historically marginalized groups because it is so normalized in circles that have power. I can't remember any time where I've talked to a white male where he's talking about sponsorship or using that language. I've heard them say I'm backing this person or I'm supporting this person, but you never hear about them talking about sponsorship as if it's a thing because it's a natural extension of what they do.

What about the other side of the coin? What makes a great protégé?

In my mind, I really see the underpinning of sponsorship is around trust and I do think that you have to deliver from your end as a protégé. As a sponsor, I'm extending my political social capital to support you, but that means you have to deliver when I put you on stretch projects. Of course, I'll support you and do everything I can to make sure you're successful, but you need to make sure that you are doing everything you need to do to execute when those opportunities are given to you. That's why I feel sponsorship is more so reserved for people that can deliver. I won't say "high performing" because I think sometimes it's hard to parse between if you have the core capabilities to do work and you just didn't have the opportunity to do said work. That could be why you're not considered to be "high performing." I do think the desire and willingness to execute to your highest capability is important. I also think that you have to set up the sponsor to be able to speak about you in places where you're not, so the sponsor needs to really understand what your career aspirations are. What are the skills you have to offer? I think they have to know how they can help you. When those opportunities are afforded you have to be ready to deliver.

How did you approach obtaining a sponsor?

I have never been the person that's actively seeking these things. I've never been the person to seek out someone to be my sponsor. These relationships developed generally from people that I've worked with or had enough interaction with. They have trust in my ability to deliver and a level of confidence in me based on previous work. My style is much more organic, and I don't feel that I've ever actively tried to get a sponsor. I think that's just my personality, it comes more naturally from me.

This book focuses on inclusive sponsorship. How have you either experienced or observed inequity in gaining access to sponsors?

When I hear this question, I think about seeing certain groups of people getting access to sponsors more so than others. Yes, I definitely had seen it when I was a consultant. There is one CEO that I worked with that had this Saturday biking crew that would bike all the time. There were a few people on the team that were also bikers. Granted, they were all old white men, and many of them knew the CEO personally. It was well known that this was the biking crew and that those were *his* people and so I think it created a tight circle of trust that was hard to penetrate if you didn't fit the mold. If you didn't want to spend your weekends with this group or perhaps you don't even like biking, then how do you compete with those that do? You won't get the same access to the CEO as those that were in this biking crew. Oftentimes, I have seen how social situations create those relationships and then you know how to position yourself for the right opportunities. In those social situations, you will get implicit insight into new projects that most people don't know about. A sponsor might say, "Let me email this person to connect you on this top-secret project" an executive is working on. It's in those social situations where these types of conversations happen—usually away from the office, somewhere private. It is certainly inequitable, especially in this hybrid environment where you start to have some people that are in person and some that are not. I was in a meeting today and there were three people in the room together and then three of us connecting virtually on a computer screen. The people in the room were having side conversations and building relationships while those that were connecting virtually didn't have that benefit. The people in the room were starting to build trust and then also having this space to actually talk about the meeting and other important aspects of the project together. Even in these in-person conversations, quick connections to other colleagues can be made because you have that common space together and dedicated time to connect. I have also seen inequities with how high-profile projects are assigned. Sometimes when a team doesn't have a process on how to assign these projects, it becomes up to the individual leader to ensure that all team members have opportunities. What I've seen is that the leader or individual only thinks who is top of mind and who they've connected with for those opportunities.

Case Study #1 Key Takeaways

Jill's experience is certainly not a singular one for women of color. Her experience as a Black consultant at one of the largest consulting firms is similar, quite frankly, to mine. She used the quality of the projects that she worked on to drive sponosrship relationships organically. Those relationships felt more enriching and natural to her. Her work product allowed her to get selected for even more high-visibility work. This drives home the point of what it means to be sponsor-ready, which we'll talk about in chapter 8. For you to attract sponsors, they have to have comfort in your abilities. Without strong evidence of your ability to perform at a high level, many sponsors will be reluctant to put their name behind you. I also found fascinating the issue of inequity around in-person versus virtual relationships, which certainly skyrocketed during the pandemic. Her perception on the ease by which the sponsor-protégé relationship can flourish if there are more in-person interactions is an astute one. It also means that sponsors will need to be even more mindful about how to engage with future protégés as organizations transition to the hybrid environment. Setting up virtual watercooler conversations with your protégés or even using texting to stay connected are great ways to continue communicating with one another and checking in to see how the sponsor and protégé are doing. Protégés need to know that you care about their well-being in addition to being able to support their career aspirations.

Case Study 2: Sponsorship to me means psychological safety as a woman of color.[3]
    I met Layla when she worked for Management Leadership for Tomorrow (MLT), an organization that helps prepare underrepresented minorities for top business schools across the United States. Currently, Layla, an Afro-Latina, works in inclusion, diversity, and equity (ID&E) at a large tech company and is also self-publishing a book on her life story. I sat down with Layla to hear her perspectives on sponsorship. I was keen on interviewing Layla for a few reasons. Not only is she an up-and-comer, but she has a unique perspective as a woman of color from multiple intersectionalities. Layla grew up in a low-income neighborhood and made her way to matriculating at one the most well-known and respected Ivy League MBA programs in the world. Her knowledge, experience, toughness, and perseverance landed her roles at organizations such as Merrill Lynch and Beckman Coulter. I was curious to know how her lived experiences have impacted her sponsorship relationships and how these relationships should look different for women of color. Here is her perspective.

When you hear the word *sponsorship*, **what does that look like and mean to you?**

The most important thing that it feels like is psychological safety. You know you've got cover. What it looks like is basically having the ability to talk to someone about something that is risky to you and them holding the line for you. It could be risky and could be very great. As a sponsor I'm supporting you on the downside along with the upside.

How do you differentiate between mentorship and sponsorship?

Mentorship is "here's what you can do" and "here's what I would recommend." It's all on you to move things forward. With sponsorship, it feels like more of a shared responsibility. As a sponsor, I'm going to "move the pieces" so that you can succeed. I'm going to elevate you on the upside and protect you on the downside. A sponsor says, "I got you."

What characteristics do you feel make a great sponsor?

The number one thing is courage, especially in relation to how this person assumes being a "playmaker" for you. It takes courage—more often or not, it's easy for people to go with the status quo and not ruffle any feathers. Another is self-awareness. You have to know where you are positioned and help others see how they're positioned so that they can make moves.

What characteristics do you feel make a great protégé?

As a protégé, one hard-learned lesson for me: you have to know when you just need to fall in line. There's information that sometimes your sponsor can't give you. You also have to be super agile, coachable, and proactive. Your sponsor should never be guessing or wondering what you're going to do or if you will follow through. They shouldn't be concerned that they will toss the ball to you to make a "play" and that you will drop the ball. You have to show up. Essentially, you are your sponsor—you are a reflection of your sponsor, and this has to be on your mind at all times.

Have you ever experienced or observed inequity in gaining access to sponsors in your career?

Yes, there are inequities. If you are a part of a development program, getting sponsors is a piece of cake. I'm also keenly aware, having gone to Harvard Business School (HBS), that people are attracted to this. They are more likely to take an interest and sponsor me because I went to HBS and I'm Afro-Latina so that they can hang their hat on this. So, I know even from an educational background, there are inequities where people gravitate to professionals that came from a certain educational pedigree. I think it also depends on the leadership of the organization and whether you have opportunities to get visibility through the work that you do. I'll give you the example of an accountant that sits behind a desk reconciling books. They are rarely in the strategy meetings where the heavy-hitting executives are, planning for the year, and slotting people into different projects. That accountant does great work but doesn't have the visibility to even get a sponsor. Their manager might not even be senior enough either to get a sponsor. The biggest inequity, I feel, is that you are less likely to be sponsored if your direct manager has never experienced sponsorship. If they haven't experienced it and felt it, then they don't know how to be a sponsor for others. In addition to this, that manager might even discourage that accountant from seeking sponsorship themselves because it might be threatening to them or perceived as taking away from the work you do for them.

How should sponsorship look and feel different for women of color?

As a sponsor, you need to be willing to hold space for and acknowledge that there are very real visible and invisible personal and institutional barriers that play into our experiences. There has to be room to understand and validate the lived experiences of women of color. Above all else is not questioning, explaining away, or rationalizing our experiences. It can feel very alienating and can create distance and misunderstanding. There also has to be an intimate understanding of what the barriers are for women of color. There needs to be humility that you might not understand. You have to be willing to ask the question to the protégé and say, "I might not understand your experience. That said, what would support look like for you?" You have to let the protégé *be the author* of what that support should be.

If you could sit down with the CEO or C-Suite at one of the top companies in the world, what do you feel they need to know about sponsorship broadly or even in the organization?
The most important thing they need to know is that sponsorship, mentorship, peer coaching—these need to be foundational to whether or not people get promoted to leadership positions. Sponsorship needs to be baked into how we lead and do business. If we aspire to be the world's best employer, this is nonnegotiable. The second thing I would say is that I need senior leadership to develop a degree of comfort with the discomfort they will feel about telling people that have historically had sponsorship to "have a seat. Right now, it's not about them." As you talk about sponsorship and mentorship or anytime you talk about advancing someone's career, inevitably, other folks raise their hand and say, "Me too, me too." This is especially true when the discussion is about advancing people of color. As with any other business problem where we are focusing on a certain population or challenge, there needs to be a well-thought-out commitment to see the action plan through and a communication plan that really drives the message home about why we are focusing on people of color at this time. Think about it in the context of business opportunities. We would never allow this scope creep to happen. If we said we are going to do an analysis to evaluate which market to penetrate next with a new product, we would never abandon that market strategy midway through execution in service of expanding it so it can be inclusive of another market. It doesn't make any sense. We win by employing thoughtful, focused, clearly defined strategies. Regrettably, we give ourselves all kinds of leeway when it comes to people issues, and the lack of rigor around driving accountability only compounds the matter.

How would you recommend leadership deal with these sorts of issues around strategy to expand sponsorship for people of color?

I would say—as with any other business challenge—develop a strategy and execute it. Do not be hesitant about clearly addressing that in Year 1 or Year 2, the focus will be on women of color and that you will iterate from there based on what you learn. Reiterate the focus at every turn because realistically, you're not going to get anywhere if you try to boil the ocean and address everything at once. Leaders are trained on how to do this—how to communicate within the organization that there are certain priorities that leadership is focused on for a predetermined period of time. Unfortunately, in my experience, when it comes to people-related issues, we lose the rigor and execution excellence we often see in the core business. I get that it can be uncomfortable to look folks who are not used to hearing "no" or "not right now" in the eye and effectively telling them "not right now." This can be tricky and very frustrating for the workforce. Developing a communication strategy around that with your HR partners is crucial to being successful here.

What else would you say to senior leadership about sponsorship? How do you think they can show up as sponsors?

The number-one thing I would say is to show your work. Make it visible. Who are your protégés? What are they achieving? Share those stories. Also, if you are leading an organization, you have the ability to drastically improve the quality of relationships your workforce has with each other, which can dramatically improve your bottom line. Think about going into business with someone that you really care about. You enjoy the work. You enjoy each other. Work turns into happy hour. Happy hour turns into weekend vacations, which turn into entire monthly retreats. There's an X factor about fostering these types of connections and relationships that has a multiplier effect.

Case Study #2 Key Takeaways

Layla pointed out that for women of color, sponsorship could mean psychological safety, especially when you are working in an environment where you as the protégé may not know who to trust. And there is a very special role for sponsors of women of color. In addition to creating that safe space, you have to be willing to not just listen to but accept the lived experiences of Black and Brown women in your place of work. That's where relationship development can begin, and for some women of color, this is a nonstarter. It's difficult to develop an authentic relationship with a sponsor who is combative or unwilling to accept their lived experience as fact. Finally, for organizations that are trying to increase sponsorship for women of color, don't be afraid to communicate this message within your organization. Craft the story by being transparent about the data regarding women of color, whether it's attrition, number of women of color at the manager level or higher, or employee-satisfaction ratings. Tie the data to the *why* on the importance on focusing on this population to move the organization forward.

Case Study #3: Playing the social game to find sponsors hits differently for women of color.[4]

Another eye-opening conversation occurred with Anika, a Black female senior executive who is now a regional VP for a publicly traded managed-care company. I asked her to join my conversations around sponsorship because I knew she had a unique perspective on how it impacted her journey. A registered nurse (RN) by training and a guru in clinical informatics, she created a different path for herself, where she now focuses on using data to improve patient, provider, and employee journeys throughout the healthcare ecosystem. She talks about her definition of sponsorship and how social dynamics have impacted how she interacts with sponsors to achieve her career goals. She also delves into a topic that I personally don't believe gets a lot of airplay as it relates to the realities of sponsorship—how your socioeconomic status plays into the spaces you get to occupy as both a sponsor and a protégé.

What does sponsorship look like and feel like to you?

That's a really good question. I think my experience in management consulting, more so than anything, has impacted my viewpoints on sponsorship. Inside management-consulting culture, there was an annual process we would go through as managers and senior managers to decide our counselees' (typically consultants and senior consultants) year-end rating. You all get into a room where you would represent your counselees, and you would stand up and you'd speak about their accomplishments. All counselees would be put on a scale from 1 to 5 and then you would literally hash out the ratings. Honestly, I think of sponsorship as a person that would bang the table for you when you are not in the room.

I think over time, probably as I've grown, that picture has shifted to where I understand more about the pre-meeting and the post-meeting than I did when I was at in management consulting. Coming to Intermountain Healthcare, the pre-meeting and post-meeting really magnified the extension of political capital, the introductions, the dinners you probably wouldn't have been invited to, so that you can have visibility. I really think that continues to permeate my thinking about sponsorship. Whenever someone asks me this question, I still envision my experience in management consulting—the partner banging the table for you in that room trying to advocate for you and making sure your year-end rating is appropriate, but I also recognize there is a much more nuanced component as well.

Could you expand on the pre- and post-meeting that you talked about? I think this is a really important point.
    I definitely think it is always about the pre-meeting, the offer to assist in ways that are often not tied directly to your responsibilities. One of the biggest sponsors that I had at Intermountain, the first time I met her I was a consultant in a completely different capacity. She invited me to breakfast, and over the meeting she asked me some questions. She asked me, "If you were designing an organization, what would that look like?" And I literally drew it on a napkin. After that meeting, she catapulted my career at Intermountain. She connected me with another colleague because she liked my ideas and we connected at a restaurant. It's the breakfast meeting, it's the dinner meeting. It's the Christmas party at so and so's house. People underestimate the power of being likable and being liked; it breeds connection. It is so important to any individual's career. I know how

hard that can be to grapple with and to understand. Oftentimes, especially for people of color, you feel like some of the things we talk about more openly now—the code-switching, the malleability, and ignoring micro aggressions—become more and more necessary to be liked. I was very fortunate early in my career. I was a traveling critical care nurse; a Jamaican woman gave me my first promotion into administration. She introduced me to the business of healthcare, how money moves within the business. I consider her to be the first leader to give me life lessons about leadership. She taught me the lessons that only a Black woman would tell another Black woman. I could not begin to describe the impact of that experience on my career and my growth. It was the small things—she talked about the tradeoffs that you have to make. These are the doors that you have to get into if you want to hit this milestone in your career. Make no mistake that this is how you will always be perceived, but that doesn't matter. It's more about how you see yourself.

I would also admit that I was fortunate to have my career experience on the West Coast. I grew up in the Southeast, and this was the first time that I'd felt people really valued something over skin color. On the West Coast, it was always about money and relationships. It was the first time that I saw how *green* overcame *Brown*. It meant that demonstrating my value could overcome the barriers that were presented to me in the South and the Southeast. I found myself at twenty-seven years old as a critical care manager at a very large hospital. There was no way on God's green earth this would happen in South Carolina, where I'm from. And then I went up the ladder from manager to senior director.

How have you experienced mentorship and sponsorship in your career?

I often think of mentorship as more educational and guidance, but traditionally my experience has been: when I had a mentor, that person is providing guidance, but the aspect of improvement (the work of improvement) lies with the mentee. I think of mentorship in that way. My COO at Intermountain became my mentor. One of the first things he asked me to do was develop a career plan, and I had never developed one before. I never paused to say to myself, "What do I *want* to do?" Doing that was an awesome experience, and he was a great mentor. The difference would be in a mentor-mentee relationship is that I developed that plan, brought it back to him, and he gave me some coaching on my plan and areas that I should think about with more intent. In a sponsorship conversation, I probably would have said, "I don't know that I've ever felt privileged enough to document on paper what I want to do." As a next step, I would have probably been looking for: now that I have written these things down, how are you going to help me actually open these doors and walk through them. To me, that's the difference. I don't want to undervalue a mentor because the person is giving you their time and that's one of the greatest gifts anyone could ever give you. With sponsorship, they are extending political capital and inviting you into spaces. They are *specifically looking for opportunities* for your growth and giving you the experience you need to move forward.

For example, in a mentor relationship, if you really want said opportunity and you showed your mentor said job description, the mentor will say, "See if you could connect with that person on LinkedIn." "See if you can reach out and get a coffee meeting." A sponsor would say "I believe I know someone that can help you get in the door. Let me reach out and set up a meeting so that you can learn more."

What characteristics do you feel make a great sponsor?

The biggest thing is that the sponsor needs to be invested, really invested in seeing their protégé's growth and development. In full transparency, they need to be positioned in a place where they can provide assistance. The relationship and connection between the sponsor and the person they are working with needs to lend toward that desire and investment in wanting to see that person move forward so that you can open doors for them. A sponsor probably has to understand the value of relationships in a nuanced way. I had this as an interview question once: "What is a lesson that you learned in your career that you didn't learn in college?" I said, "The value of relationships." We talked about networking, but it was one of those things that was sort of calculated and purposeful—getting on a project, getting on a proposal, getting the right rating. The long-term relationships that circle back, the kind of relationships that you can come back to, sponsors are really great at navigating these types of longitudinal relationships. They understand business relationships that can be extended in the service of others. It becomes a tighter network with lots of connections, and it is also a network where you can ask for grace when you make business mistakes. I am super high on grace. It is one of those gifts that we give to people and one that people tend not to admit when they need it. As a sponsor, you need to understand where your safe spaces are to have that type of career growth.

What would make a great protégé?

I'd also say investment here as well. There has to be a deep desire for attainment, whatever that looks like for the protégé. Whatever we are working on together, we should have a shared understanding about our desires to get there. Also, be honest about what you do and don't want done on your behalf or extension of you. Be comfortable having that conversation. I used to say to my sponsor, "I would not stab someone in the back to get a certain opportunity." That's not part of who I am, and it's not authentic to how I show up as a leader. Also, be targeted and have a map of experiences that you would like to have, and here are the areas on the map where I would want the sponsor to help me. Be consistent in reaching out to your sponsor and keep them apprised of what you need. Executives are very busy, so always feel free to continue to reach out to your sponsor. Don't leave them in the dark. Finally, think about what your tradeoff is going to be. Usually, mentorship and sponsorship are a gift, they are probably doing that because they are seeing some value in you. Think about how you can leverage that value for your mentor or your sponsor.

Have you observed or experienced inequity in gaining sponsors?

Oh, for sure. When I was in Utah, it was a homogenous population, so I stood out from that perspective. There was also a majority religion, so I also stood out there as well. All of these things culminated in access to sponsors looking different for me. People who were meeting sponsors were meeting at ice cream socials by the church or during church service or at other events that I wouldn't naturally attend. Don't get me wrong, I had amazing sponsors at Intermountain, but it came by me differently. It didn't come through relationships or simply occupying space as it would to others. The sponsors came through my work, not socially. I've overheard colleagues say they had sponsors because their parents knew an executive's cousin and they sat together at church. Or they say my parents brought me to charity events where we occupied the same space with executive leadership. It comes naturally to the sponsor in these social settings to build desire to see the children of friends succeed. It is so inherently difficult for women of color. I'm a first-generation college graduate, and my husband and I talk about it all the time. The friends and network that we are building now will help support our children's growth that are in businesses, industries, and sectors that we aren't in. These are the things we didn't have growing up. Figuring out how to occupy these spaces, getting that invitation to that Christmas party that only certain people know about. We are, interestingly, having to do the work of networking into the social spaces where we need to be.

I also think it's the comfort when you do get into the space. The inequity also comes with the level of comfort you have when you get there. I mean I took my first class on etiquette in high school (governor's school), then others in both college and grad school. My husband has a very different job than I do, but we tend to network together. I served on a governor's commission in Utah, so we would go out to dinners and other types of networking events (most others would have just considered them social outings). One time I got invited to Park City for a ski weekend our CFO holds, a super exclusive invite. We often would come from a weekend like this, and I would need several days of downtime. My husband would look at me and say, "But we just came from a ski weekend, why do you need a break?" And I would turn to him and say, "this was *work* for me." Let me be clear. For everyone else, it was fun, but for me it was work. This is another inequity that I don't think is talked about among women of color—the exhaustion that comes from having to be *on* all the time in social settings. Make no mistake—this was not like me and my husband going away for a ski weekend, and I come downstairs in my PJs for breakfast. This is very different. Additionally, the other inequity is that these are new experiences for many of us. We can't relate to being whisked away for a ski weekend. I have to stop myself at some of these events from saying "my goodness, people live like this?" "This is what people do every day?" I didn't even know.

Case Study #3 Key Takeaways

One of the most important nuggets I took away from our conversation is that as a woman of color, networking to find sponsors absolutely feels like work. I can't remember a time when I went to a dinner with my boss or other senior executives and truly let my guard down. Not that I would completely abandon my manners or professionalism, never. It's the feeling that I'm doubly under a microscope being Black and being a woman. I feel that I have to overthink what I say and how I behave in the presence of my colleagues and peers. God forbid I make a mistake, tell a joke that didn't land, or even wear my natural hair; those mistakes would be scrutinized more than anyone else's. I also empathized with her sentiments on how she grew up and how that affects her ability to feel comfortable in certain social settings. Admittedly, I grew up middle class, but it always sends me into an internal panic if I get invited for an afternoon on a senior leader's boat or visit their home for the first time. The first time this happened, a part of me felt a bit of shame that I had never experienced stepping into a lavish mansion before or that I wasn't privately tutored in school. As sponsors, you might have protégés who came from more humble beginnings and can't swap stories with you about the summer vacations to the Hamptons you used to take. It's important to understand that your protégé may have different life goals that include more family interaction and work-life balance versus more money or material possessions. Getting to know your protégé's personal goals in addition to their professional ones is important to deepening the relationship.

5

POWER DYNAMICS
IN SPONSORSHIP

One of my most treasured moments in the last two years was being a part of the leadership team responsible for launching the first Business Resource Group (BRG) for Black Women at Atrium Health. The BRG, named A²WeXcel, was designed to give African American and Black women a safe place to network, learn more about career development in healthcare, and give back to Black-led organizations in the Charlotte community. It took years, even decades, for this BRG to finally come to fruition. Several Black female leaders had attempted to start a similar group, but unfortunately did not receive executive support at that time. Other BRGs existed for Black men, veterans, and the LGBTQ+ communities within the organization—but none for Black women. It wasn't until a senior-leadership turnover that resulted in a new chief executive officer and new chief people officer being installed did this initiative move forward. I would also be remiss not to mention the courage and determination of several strong Black female executives without whom this initiative would not have been possible, namely Monifa Drayton, Kinsey Evans, and Tracie Taylor. Their continued vigilance to ensure that this BRG got the attention and prominence it deserved is not only appreciated but celebrated by myself and others. The kickoff, which happened in February 2020, was met with great success, and infused not only a sense of belonging but also a commitment to seeing Black women succeed within the organization. Several months after its launching, A²WeXcel introduced rich educational programming, to include a mentorship program that allowed Black female colleagues to get to know one another, in many cases for the first time. This initiative certainly moved the organization in the right direction along its diversity, equity, and inclusion journey. However, little did I know, there was still more work to do to better understand the needs of Black female leaders.

On July 20, 2020, I hosted a Zoom community call with a group of Black female vice presidents who were members of A²WeXcel, and we explored the topic of career sponsorship and what it should look like within our organization. It was an enlightening conversation, and one that took me by surprise. One of the questions I opened the discussion with was "What does sponsorship look like to you in your careers?" The common themes emerged again: Sponsorship relationships developed over time. It took multiple tries to find the right sponsor that would advocate for them. They have seen their white and/or male colleagues who did not appear to work as hard, gain sponsors at a faster rate. As I skimmed my laptop screen, I saw several heads nodding in agreement, although there was still a sense of silence on the call. And then there were a few women who offered a contrary opinion. One executive chimed in and said that she didn't see the value in actively pursuing sponsorship. She said she had mostly focused on keeping her head down and doing exceptional work. Doing so worked for her, and while she may not have gotten promoted with the same speed as her colleagues, she still eventually was promoted. I could see the silent gasps on my screen. Then another more senior Black female executive stated that she didn't need sponsorship at that juncture in her career. She wasn't looking for a promotion or further advancement. She simply wanted to come in to work, do a good job, and serve as a mentor for other rising leaders. There was a short discussion by sponosrship advocates on the call that attempted to reinforce the importance of sponsorship, but you could see that there was clearly a new dynamic among the group—women that supported actively pursuing sponsorship and women who didn't see it as being necessary. Several of our colleagues truly believed that focusing on the work was the most direct route to getting promoted.

In addition to these new viewpoints on sponsorship, it was also apparent on the call that we didn't really know one another and what we do. At the top of the discussion when introducing ourselves, there were ladies on the call whom I'd never met that were doing wonderful things within the organization and the community. One thing gnawing at me was that if I didn't know some of these fantastic women, then other senior leaders probably didn't, either. If our paths didn't cross through our work or even after work, we were missing opportunities to connect and support each other's career goals. Perhaps we needed to encourage Black female leaders in A²WeXcel to introduce themselves to each other and to other executives within the organization. What better way to begin advocating for yourself than with a quick PowerPoint slide on who you are and what your career goals are, and to highlight some of the projects and initiatives that are your proudest accomplishments. We also included a few statistics at the beginning of the PowerPoint deck that oriented the reader around the opportunity to support Black women and career advancement, specifically the percentage of Black women currently at the executive level, educational degrees received, and the average tenure overall for Black women. In a sense, this served as a business case for supporting Black women's advancement. We compiled these slides into a "Facebook" of sorts that could be shared if you're meeting a new leader, want to set up an introductory coffee with a colleague, or simply have a resource that could serve as your elevator pitch. After introducing the concept to the group, some ladies were eager to participate and put their Facebook slide together, and others didn't respond at all. I compiled the slides as a draft document from the women that completed them and shared them with our BRG's executive sponsor as a heads-up. She thought this would be an excellent resource and didn't see any issues with the content that each professional put on their slide. It was empowering and we honestly gleaned new insights from the exercise. I learned that several ladies had received powerful national awards for their work in clinical quality. I learned that a few women went to the same alma mater as I did or grew up near the same hometown. Most importantly, I learned what they wanted to achieve in their careers, whether it was being a leader in health equity or wanting to run a hospital one day. The exercise allowed me to understand, empathize, and connect on a new level with other Black women.

And yet, I was surprised again. After the draft document was completed and shared with only our executive sponsor, I received texts and phone calls from members of the A²WeXcel leadership team with concerns they were hearing about the exercise. Mind you, the document had only been shared with one person, but we all know how these sorts of things get legs. The concerns weren't coming from white leaders that might have seen the document as a preview. The concerns were raised by Black women that were asked to complete it as an exercise. What I heard baffled me. Some of the ladies did not want to be associated with the initiative for fear that they would be "labeled" as a troublemaker within the enterprise. Others were concerned that this initiative would be viewed as Black women trying to organize or stage an intervention with senior leadership that would be met with swift denouncement. And a few women felt that including their PowerPoint slides would jeopardize promotion opportunities that were currently "in the works" for them. Who would have thought that putting together a set of profile slides would set in motion a wave of concerns that essentially was the antithesis of the intent of the initiative? But their concerns shouldn't be downplayed or ignored. While I was frustrated and saddened by their responses, especially as a proponent of sponsorship, I appreciated their candor and feedback. If anything, it unearthed a reality for Black and Brown women, at every organization regardless or title or tenure. The underlying issue is the power dynamics at play and the belief that a Black woman's career is in the hands of someone else. And that as a woman of color, you are not in control of your own professional destiny. Even if you work hard and do all the right things, how you are perceived by white colleagues can either accelerate or decelerate your potential. I wouldn't even call this an unease with being associated with diversity initiatives and programs. It is a downright fear by association, particularly if your superior is white. Mind you, the PowerPoint slides were not circulated to anyone outside of the BRG and our executive sponsor. But just the thought that their boss or their boss's boss would see their profile and have a negative reaction was enough for several women to immediately opt out.

This story underscores some of the power and social dynamics that women of color experience in their work environments. The spectrum of these lived experiences has shaped women of color's viewpoints on being sponsored and provides additional color to the challenges executives and organizations may have to face in advancing sponsorship for Black and Brown women. Sponsorship, stripped down to its basic and fundamental parts, is an important mechanism to promote women of color, as it allows leaders to use their political and social capital for the good of the individual being sponsored as well as the organization. But what happens when this power and its use are shrouded in fear? How can women of color understand who holds social and political power within their organizations and how power is exchanged? What do we do as leaders when we know power inequities exist, and our most marginalized employees are the ones that bear the brunt? Most importantly, how does playing the social game and understanding power dynamics impact the ability of women of color to be sponsored in their career?

To explore this further, I sat down with a couple of colleagues to get their take on the power dynamics affecting sponsorship for women of color. The lessons derived from these conversations can be helpful for organizations looking to invest further in diverse talent and for Black and Brown professionals hoping to understand how to navigate sponsorship for themselves.

A conversation about power dynamics in sponsorship.

To explore the topics on power more candidly and deeply, I went to the source. One of my favorite conversations regarding sponsorship was with a white male colleague of mine, Doug Riddle, a senior fellow and senior portfolio advisor for Leadership Solutions with the Center for Creative Leadership.[1] He is also the curriculum director for the Carol Emmott Foundation and has a deep passion for coaching women of color and professionals from underrepresented groups. I had always been impressed with Doug and his boldness around the need to support and advocate for diverse women. We sat down to discuss sponsorship from his vantage point and the key issues facing leadership about advancing women of color.

Who holds the power in sponsorship?

I admit I went into this question with an assumption—particularly when people are taught about the dynamics of power. Doug felt the notion that white males are somehow taught about power or how to network at a young age was not always true. In his view, it had more to do with whether you come from a family with strong political or financial means. I shared with him that in general, Black women aren't taught how to navigate power. Personally, I couldn't remember a time when a family member or a colleague told me about what power truly means in the corporate setting. What I can recall from my upbringing is my mother sitting me down, probably around age eleven, to tell me that I should always strive to be independent and have my own money. Oh, how right she was! However, most of my power and political savvy came from observation—watching how my peers built relationships and whom they decided to associate with. My general observation was that white males seemed to do this innately and effortlessly. They were getting invited to their boss's Sunday dinner, which you found out about after the fact, where they discussed an important project that he needed help with. Or they were asked to join a group of executives for a weekend at a senior executive's lake house, and you think to yourself "I didn't even know they *had* a lake house!" My white colleagues were getting invitations to these private social engagements, but to me it felt as though they didn't even have to ask for those opportunities. The opportunities found them, and please believe that the discussions happening in these private, closed-door sessions are absolutely about you, your colleagues, your team, and the business as a whole.

I boldly told Doug that I assumed that white males are taught how to navigate these situations. They probably had someone early on, be it a mentor or simply a more seasoned professional that connected with them on a personal level, that was watching out for them. Someone took an interest in them early because they grew up in the same hometown, went to the same church, or were huge fans of the same football team. He immediately agreed with my premise, but disagreed with the notion that guys, and white males especially, were being taught overtly about power. In fact, he shared that in his experience, it's extremely rare. From his calculation, you might find that 90 percent of men aren't taught unless they come from extreme wealth or generational power. We are talking about the type of power and wealth that is inherited, passed down, and treasured. Most people of color, particularly in the United States, have never experienced this type of power. To my surprise, Doug asserted that learning about power happens much more organically for men. You'll see this theme several times in this book—the organic nature of how sponsorship happens. But power, Doug believes, might actually be more directly related to socioeconomic status. "If you come from a family with power, you know how to keep it," he says. "If you're birthed into an environment of relative power, people inherit those rules and learn them from the beginning." And these individuals go on to run some of the biggest corporations and tend to surround themselves with other people that grew up the same way. In listening to Doug talk, it felt like he was describing belonging to a secret society where the rules about power are very implicit. The question becomes, How do we make the rules of power explicit, particularly in the corporate environment? And how do we change those rules specifically to give access to powerful and influential sponsors for diverse talent?

Doug pointed me to a book written in 2017 called *The Influence Effect: A New Path to Power for Women Leaders*. The premise of the book is that what works for men vis-à-vis political savvy won't necessarily work for women. The book challenges traditional thinking around how women gain power and specifically provides five strategies for gaining influence: the power of the informal, relationship maps, scenario thinking, influence loops, and momentum. It creates a framework for how women can create their own rules for gaining power in a corporate environment using smart approaches to win.[2] I would venture even further that the nuances related to political savvy and power for women of color are also drastically different. I reflected on the conversations I had with rising women of color executives and found that the approach to building relationships is significantly overlayed with perceptions about race. Having to also be aware of and fight against stereotypes while trying to develop relationships on a more informal, social level is fraught with continued struggles and fatigue. Sponsorship is critical in helping women of color gain power because of the power and influence a sponsor has to help provide additional visibility.

Why do organizations struggle with sponsorship for women of color?

Corporations, and especially the executives leading them, know what sponsorship is. Many have been sponsored themselves, although they might have a different terminology or definition for how they've been advocated for and supported throughout their career. If they collectively understand the importance of sponsorship from their lived experiences, why is it so difficult for organizations to successfully sponsor women of color? The fascinating part of our conversation occurred when we talked about the abundance of corporations that have created formal programs for sponsorship. Surprisingly though, Doug felt that these sorts of programs could be potentially dangerous to achieving the outcomes that organizations desire around diversity. In his opinion, it is a two-edged sword for affirmative action. It is a way to quickly demonstrate the organization's commitment to diversity by showcasing to employees that there is a formalized program to address these needs. However, what women of color, and diverse professionals in general, want is for the behaviors of management and leadership to inherently change and work better. In fact, Doug challenges the common thinking around developing sponsorship programs because they lack the specificity on the dynamics of what takes place to make this type of meaningful change. A sponsorship program can only be as good as the outcomes it produces. For example, if a company decides to sponsor ten Black female managers, how many of these managers were promoted at the conclusion of the program? How many new executive relationships was the protégé able to develop as a result of their participation? What high-visibility initiatives was the protégé selected for that can be directly tied back to their sponsor's advocacy of their selection? What tends to happen is that there is high engagement by both the sponsor and protégé at the beginning of the program and relationship, with no conclusion or outcome. But because there was high engagement, companies consider that to be a positive sign that the program was successful and should be continued. This leads organizations to be hypocritical around the intent behind diversity and inclusion and to make declarative statements about their support of diversity without the true outcomes to prove their actions were sincere.

The other challenge, and ugly truth, about the lack of success with sponsorship programs is that companies suffer from placing the blame on the "victim," in this case, the protégé. Doug states, "We are dominated by an individualistic society and unfortunately we expect Black women to figure out all of these things and jump through the right hoops on their own." There are no real solutions that are not predicated on group, organizational, and social dynamics. Critically important is understanding power dynamics and how social capital operates as a mechanism for power. Sponsorship is a power relationship; make no mistake, he says. The sponsor holds the power and is in a trusted position to use their power for the benefit of their protégé. On the other hand, mentoring has a paradoxical dynamic—it acknowledges someone has more overt power and theoretically is designed to give their mentees opportunities for access, but sponsorship is more about taking action.

The other, and more frank reason: Doug believes organizations struggle with sponsorship for diverse talent is that they simply don't do it. The company may periodically wake up when there is a large retirement of talent forthcoming and realize that there will be a mass exodus with no pipeline to supply new talent. But there will be very little consistency and much more sporadic attempts in what organizations will do to solve the talent problem. Additionally, efforts for sponsorship are so easily defeated because there is so little energy to make it happen. The fact is that many executives are already strapped for time. Some executives sit on multiple committees, have dozens of direct reports, and see sponsorship as something they might do if they have time. The executives who lean into sponsorship make the time. They make it a part of their core values and activities to spend time developing others. They block uninterrupted time on their Outlook calendar. They put their phone away when they are spending time with a protégé to stay focused and actively listen. The other piece to the puzzle on why more executive leaders are not sponsoring diverse talent is that the mechanisms by which you become sponsored are not widely understood. You cannot substitute the behaviors used in mentoring with sponsorship. Asking someone whom you don't already have a relationship with to sponsor you does not work. Doug likens it to someone desperate to date someone. The desperation turns you off, and this is true for executive leaders. People also get anxious when they are asked to sponsor someone since it is not normal in our society. There's no practice to draw from. "If you never ask someone out on a date, you're going to be bad at it."

Digging deeper into this topic, Doug shared the hesitancy that can be felt among the executive ranks around sponsoring talent that they don't know. "I never accepted an offer to sponsor someone that I didn't already have a relationship with." This is also true for several executive leaders I interviewed for this book. Mostly, people sponsor others that are in their orbit. They have to be close to us and, most importantly, *like* us. It is very much a perceptional reality and the way most sponsorship happens.

We delved further into the issue with companies and sponsorship. Doug believes, and I agree, that there is a potential negative impact in being designated for a sponsorship program. In essence, you are set aside as being *special* in your organization. Once you are deemed special or different, other employees may put a target on your back. You might be viewed as "untouchable," and that can create a tense dynamic within your team, your department, and across the organization. Doug described it well—as an employee in a sponsorship program, you will absolutely get support, but you could also have people that want to sabotage your experience. It's the classic haves and the have-nots. One way organizations can overcome this issue is to simply model the way when it comes to sponsorship. I'm going to make a bold statement here. You will never see more sponsorship happening across your organization than you see the C-Suite doing. Doug agreed that the upper limit to virtuous behavior in your organization is in how senior leadership behaves. If you want your organization to change its behavior, you have to model it as a senior exec. It has to be persistent, continuous, and happening all across the company.

Are women executives part of the problem?

It's a good question and a very controversial topic. Out of the thirty-plus women I interviewed for this book, 68 percent mentioned having an experience where they felt, as a Black and Brown female employee, that, specifically, white women were not actively sponsoring them. These sentiments came without my prompting for an answer. "It typically happens around your first people leader role," said Nicole, a healthcare executive with a specialty in laboratory services. "Once you start getting noticed by others for your talent, it seems that women go into fight or flight mode and simply don't want to help. There's a feeling that there are only so many seats at the table, and they have to get that seat."[3] In fact, there is a name for this phenomenon: the Queen Bee Syndrome—the behavior that female executives treat their subordinates more critically if they are female and may refuse to help other women up the ranks to preserve their place in the corporate hierarchy. There are many criticisms of this theory altogether, from the fact that even the term *Queen Bee* perpetuates stereotypes of corporate women being aggressive and assimilating to historical male traits in the workplace. But there is some truth to the notion of lack of sponsorship by white women to Black and Brown females. In the 2021 Women in the Workplace study, while 77 percent of white employees consider themselves to be allies to women of color at work, only 10 percent mentor or sponsor one or more women of color.[4] The other interesting insight from the study is that when women of color and white employees were asked to define what "allyship" looks like, there was a stark difference between how advocacy, mentorship, and sponsorship were ranked. For women of color, advocacy was ranked first, and mentorship and sponsorship were ranked fifth (out of eight). For white employees, they were ranked third and eighth respectively.

Another uncomfortable topic is the feeling of some BIPOC women that other senior BIPOC women are not showing up as sponsors, either. Nicole goes on to share that in her experience, Black female executives have shied away from sponsoring her because of the perception that they were doing so because she is Black. That perception could have a ripple effect with other executives in the organization and could damage her brand as someone that is only sponsoring Black females or trying to give them a leg up. "It feels like tough love in a lot of ways. You would think that a senior Black executive would love to sponsor a rising Black female. But the reality is that there is still a stereotype or perception around this." This might also cause Black senior leaders to sponsor rising diverse talent as silent sponsors, behind the scenes, to demonstrate their support for diverse protégés but not in a public way. I remember speaking with a colleague of mine, a senior leader at a leading national healthcare delivery network, that shared a similar perspective. Sometimes, it's better for diverse protégés to have white sponsors because a Black sponsor won't carry as much weight in those rooms where decisions are being made. "It's one thing for me to say that so and so is great, but it will only go so far if the person is Black. However, if one of my white male colleagues spoke up on their behalf there seems to be more trust and credibility in the endorsement."

SUMMARY

Power, specifically who holds power, is a dynamic in sponsorship that must be addressed to advance diversity. It's the accountability of the sponsor that holds the power to use this power for good. Sponsors should be asking themselves constantly, "What diverse professionals are you bringing forward for advancement?" "Who is next and ready for leadership roles that I can assist with getting over the finish line?" This is how you build talent in an organization. One thing organizations should be careful of is tying sponsorship to pay. It is one thing to give employees that are role modeling sponsorship in the right way an appreciation bonus or a spot award for doing so. However, if you incorporate sponsorship as an expected part of pay, leaders could exhibit bad behavior. Leaders could be incentivized to game the system and sponsor or advocate for protégés only as much as needed to get extra compensation, and not because it is truly right for the business. Selective acknowledgment and reinforcement are key, especially if the outcome results in improved diversity and inclusion within leadership positions. Finally, as leaders, don't be afraid of going to your most influential and powerful executives and asking the critical questions about who's next. Expect regular reports to senior leadership going three levels down in the organization on whether the pipeline for talent represents the diversity of your communities. Holding power requires accountability and responsibility for those that wield it.

6

THE SPONSORSHIP MANIFESTO

The day after my promotion went through, I remember waking up and feeling a weight lifted off my shoulders. It was an indescribable feeling of excitement and relief, and a sense of accomplishment that I never had before. In reflecting on my triumphs in advocating for myself and receiving the sponsorship that I felt I deserved, I wondered how many other women like me had a similar experience. How many Black women asked their bosses for a promotion and were successful? How many Latinas demanded a raise they deserved, and it actually went through? These were the thoughts swirling in my mind. How many BIPOC women had someone in their corner to support them in these requests? I was fortunate to have a senior leader as a sponsor, but we all know that sponsorship for women of color is at an all-time low. How could women like me feel that they could be successful in achieving their career dreams when they lacked sponsorship?

I do not want to be the type of executive that just talks about the need for sponsorship. I wanted the experience of writing this book to go even further in sharing ways that all executives can be sponsors in their own right. For me, this meant making my own commitments to change the narrative and the dialogue around how to increase diversity in leadership. In one of my first leadership-development programs, which I participated in more than twenty years ago, I remember one of the instructors talking about the need to model the way. If you want to create a followership and you want to make impactful change, you have to model the behaviors you expect of others. My first step would be to sponsor women in my network that I knew were doing amazing things and were sponsor-ready. I wanted to also make my commitment meaningful. I have never been known to take the easy way out or create smaller goals that were easy to achieve. I wanted this to be a movement. I wanted organizations and executives to understand that the power was in their hands to lift up women of color. Quite frankly, I wanted leaders to be held accountable for the outcomes they expected. This is how my initiative was born and is tantamount to what I truly believe in.

One of my favorite films from the 1990s, *Jerry Maguire*, introduced me to the concept of mission statements and manifestos in my teenage years. At the time, I was too young to understand the purpose or aim of a manifesto, but there was something poignant and inspiring about documenting the thoughts and behaviors that make you who you are. I've admired several companies in my life for their public stance on who they are and how that purpose permeates the entire company in who they hire and what they do. Companies like Apple that encourages consumers to *think different*, or Fiat that embraces the passion of driving with living your best life—or even Nike that has embedded its manifesto into every single shoe it sells with its powerful slogan "Just do it." As I've gone through many experiences of mentorship and sponsorship, I began to think about how I wanted to show up for protégés and how I thought sponsors should behave for theirs as well. I journaled my experience in 2019 and thought more introspectively about my beliefs in the realm of sponsorship. These ideas turned into my manifesto—a set of belief statements that encompass how I operate as a sponsor and characterize the type of sponsor I am and want to be in the future.

Professionals who choose to actively sponsor others do so because they have an internal calling to take action and help those that need it most. The reason we are dedicated supporters of sponsorship is that we know that our success is not solely due to our hard work. We know that we had visible and silent supporters helping along the way and ensuring that our voices were elevated where we did not have access. Because of this, sponsorship has been woven into the fabric of how we decide to lead. It is an active choice. We make time to sponsor others. We live by a set of principles that direct and guide our leadership behaviors around creating the next pipeline of diverse leadership. This Sponsorship Manifesto is critical to creating an atmosphere of psychological safety and access for underrepresented employees. I highly encourage executives that want to lean into becoming sponsors to think about their own beliefs and how they are living these beliefs every day for the people they look to sponsor.

BELIEVE IN POTENTIAL

Leadership potential is a concept that can be very subjective when it comes to a person's development. One organization might define it based on an employee's annual performance along with their level of emotional intelligence. Other organizations might say that leadership potential is defined by the leader's level of ambition and IQ. Research and experience also suggest that evaluating someone based on their potential could be influenced by gender or racial bias, which can be detrimental to creating parity among employees. However, it is common for executives to identify rising leaders based on a set of characteristics of their ability to perform well in the future versus solely based on what has transpired in the past. One of the fundamental beliefs, in sponsorship, is that I'm taking my limited experience with a protégé and advocating for them without having all of the data. My protégé may never have had a leadership position before, but I have seen and observed enough of their performance to bet that they will succeed in that next-level role. In my career, I have been introduced to early and mid-careerists, where my intuition told me that they had all the makings of a powerful leader. It was that gut feeling that drove my decision to invest time and energy in developing that relationship and to finding ways to advocate and take action for them. Over time, I certainly had the opportunity to see them perform and deliver high quality work, which only reconfirmed my initial impressions. Had I waited to place that bet on their success, I could have missed opportunities to support their growth. I wouldn't be living my authentic purpose by helping others succeed if I withheld my sponsorship simply because I didn't have all of the data to 100 percent know that this person would be a success.

Believing in your employees' potential can absolutely feed your pipeline and succession plans with talented professionals. This is true, especially for sponsoring women of color, due to the structural racism, gender discrimination, and unconscious bias that has transpired across corporate america. I think about the conversation I had with a colleague of mine that has achieved tremendous success since our time together in our MBA program. Nicole Jones is a managing director of global sales support for one of the most admired airline brands across the globe. To me, she is all things Black Girl Magic, and she continues to be a role model for rising executive Black women regardless of industry. She is the recipient of numerous industry awards and is also an executive coach. Both of us are proud graduates at the Goizueta Business School at Emory University, and I was keen to pick her brain about how sponsorship played a role in her career. She shared a story about how a sponsor for her encouraged and pushed her to get outside of her comfort zone to get promoted and supported her based on her potential. Here is what she had to say about that experience.

"My sponsor challenged and promoted me (my name and capabilities) for things that were not necessarily in my wheelhouse—those stretch opportunities. I went to my most recent boss and had a career-growth conversation initiated by him. I said to him that I was really good at strategy and innovation, so I wanted to look at opportunities that were in these areas. He pushed me and said that I should find an opportunity that I wasn't experienced at or that I didn't know a lot about. Recently, we had a conversation about talent in a new area of the company, and he thought I could bring a lot of value to that role. This is a long-winded way of saying that he was a great sponsor to me because he supported me for things that were not in my comfort zone, but he had the faith and trust in me to get it done."

Using potential as a gauge for being a great sponsor allows you to uncover talent in areas of your business that you may not even know exist. It is also a creative way to solve challenging talent issues by giving protégés opportunities to shine.

BE GENEROUS

One of the tenets of career sponsorship is the belief in generosity. My most fulfilling experiences as a sponsor have been in giving my time, talent, and resources for my protégé—and expecting nothing in return. I felt happier and more peaceful as an executive. I felt that I was living my professional mission when I could extend my network to another rising woman of color. I also felt that I was doing my small part in achieving better results for my organization because I was helping to fulfill its diversity strategy. And honestly, it feels damn good to see another woman of color succeed, and I was honored to be part of that story. Ask any professional who has served as a sponsor, and they will tell you how special the experience was for them. Sponsorship brings life and joy to both the sponsor and the protégé because you are working together to achieve something great. The unconditional nature of generosity is what makes it unique. There are no expectations that someone will pay you back directly. They might pay it forward or simply say thank you and take your generosity as a gift. I personally believe that sponsors who believe in being generous will have greater satisfaction and happiness in their professional careers and have stronger and deeper relationships across their network. As a proponent of well-being in the workplace, I believe generosity will also contribute to better physical and mental health.[1] I have found that my outlook on workplace competition has also changed once I adopted generosity as a sponsorship principle. One of the reasons why executives might be reluctant to sponsor rising talent is the belief that there are only so many seats at the table. The success pie, if you will, is finite. It becomes a zero-sum game. If someone succeeds, that *must* mean that someone else must fail. For example, if I sponsor my protégé, will she overtake me in my job? Will she leapfrog over me after all of the work I have put into getting where I am? Generous leaders, on the other hand, believe that the pie continues to grow. The more protégés I sponsor who become successful, the more leaders will be inspired to do the same. Generous sponsors believe that there is infinite success out there, and we each play a role in helping people be successful. We will have greater significance in our careers when we contribute to the success of others. Generosity in sponsorship takes many forms, particularly through the actions a sponsor takes. We will explore these actions in a later chapter.

TAKE RISKS

One of the other key principles in my Sponsorship Manifesto is that a sponsor has to be willing to take risks. This one is a bit of a tricky topic to discuss, mainly since I inherently have a problem with associating sponsorship with taking risks. Believe me, I get it. For the sponsor, using your social and political capital, which you have worked so hard for, can be a risky proposition. What happens if you invest in someone, and they leave your organization? What if the person you sponsor completely tanks on an assignment, and somehow your brand has been tarnished? There are so many negative scenarios that can play out in your mind and in real life. As I have mentioned before, this is one of the reasons you may see executives shy away from sponsoring protégés. There is a fear that taking the risks will boomerang for the executive if things do not pan out. This fear can be crippling for leaders. The thought of your career being derailed due to a failed sponsorship relationship can send chills down your spine.

But here is the problem with this fear of taking risks. More than likely if you are a leader, someone took a risk or even a chance on you. Your boss might have given you your first project to manage without an abundance of data to suggest that you would be successful. Or a superior might have asked you to lead a team for the first time or give a performance review for a struggling team member. In these instances, someone not only believed in your potential but also took a risk. But that person knew they would surround you with support so that you would not be left alone if things went south. Additionally, there are so many rewards to taking risks. In fact, let's change our language on this topic. It's less about risk taking and more about *investing in people*. And what is the purpose of investing? Planting the seeds and showing your commitment to a person's professional development for future success. For example, investing your time in a Black female manager on her first leadership project can give her the confidence to take on the next opportunity and apply her learnings. Your sponsorship of her can help her do her best work by combining your generosity with the power of your advocacy. The pace of business won't allow companies to take a stepwise approach to staying competitive, and withholding your sponsorship could jeopardize opportunities for your organization to put diverse professionals in leadership roles that will augment top- and bottom-line growth.

I know what you might be thinking here. Shouldn't I be discerning in whom I decide to sponsor? Again, what if it backfires? What if she is not ready for sponsorship, and I put my name behind her? These are valid questions, and I explored these in my interview with an executive that had this experience. Ashley is a senior vice president at Bank of America Private Bank and a proud graduate of her alma mater, a historically Black college.[2] Our conversation was very enlightening. She had experience sponsoring talent, putting their names in rooms they didn't have access to. She has elevated her "right hand," an up-and-comer, and has introduced her to working relationships that led to career growth. However, she admits that she has also been burned, trusting too much in someone's intent to do good work and shine. Ashley's a big advocate of diversity and shared an example of a time where she sponsored an intern, and it did not go well.

"We had a guy that probably wasn't a great fit from my university, Jackson State, but I was so keen on getting him into the company. I will tell you that I had to call so many people just to get him into the interview process. I really put my neck out there for this guy. He ultimately got the job, and he fizzled out on me. My heart was incredibly broken, and I thought I would lose credibility.

But you learn the lessons from this experience. You pick up on the signs. You'll be able to determine if they have the same level of grit and determination needed to sponsor someone. You take the rain with the sunshine."

I was immediately intrigued to hear more. I asked her what the outcome was and how this sponsorship experience impacted her within her organization.

She went on, "I had to do some damage control. I'm not going to lie to you. I had very direct conversations with my mentors about how to navigate this and process it. And they said, you have to own it and share that you're still learning about how to identify talent. It was 100% me owning the fact that I made a mistake. And you'll find some sponsors that won't own the mistake. They will completely trash the person that they sponsored and put the onus and accountability on that protégé. But that's not my approach. I didn't have to do any extra work to make up for the fact that this person didn't work out. I had already established myself. Most of the time, my credibility outweighed any damage that came from that sponsorship relationship."

In effect, Ashley focused on being true to her authentic leadership and was able to own the unfortunate results of that sponsorship experience with her peers and superiors. She owned her role as a sponsor and used what she learned about how to spot talent to see potential red flags with protégés going forward. It is always possible that sponosrship relationships do not work out. The truth is that there aren't any guarantees that if you sponsor someone, they will succeed. But good sponsors, even great sponsors, are willing to continue to invest in talent as part of their leadership approach.

SPONSOR DIVERSE TALENT

It's not enough to be a sponsor. You should endeavor to be an *inclusive* sponsor. In practice, this means that a leader with power and influence should be equitable in using their capital for protégés across genders, ethnicities, races, and sexual orientations. The reason it is important to point out inclusivity in sponsorship is that sponsorship is a professional-development approach that is laden with bias. Sponsors naturally gravitate toward protégés who look like them because there is a commonality or a connection that makes the relationship seem more trusting. If my protégé and I had gone to the same undergraduate school, we could have conversations about our favorite courses or professors or even swap stories about the sporting events we used to attend. It feels organic and natural, and as humans we tend to layer those commonalities with perceptions about the protégé as an employee or professional. If she went to the same school as I did, she must be smart or a hard worker. If we grew up in the same town or went to the same church, she must have the same values or core principles as I do. In succumbing to this sameness paradox, we close the door on diverse talent that is not only more than capable but in need of advocacy to reach the next rung on the corporate ladder.

And it's not simply about sponsoring diverse talent. You should aim to sponsor *junior diverse talent*. Here's the reason: the glass ceiling is different based on your gender and race. For Black and Brown women, you start to feel the glass ceiling at the manager level within an organization. McKinsey and LeanIn.org discussed this in their 2019 Women in the Workplace study and put a name to it: "the broken rung." According to their research, for every 100 men promoted to management from 2018 to 2019, only 68 Latinas and 58 Black women received promotions.[3] With fewer and fewer women of color climbing the corporate ladder, it is important to invest in that talent as they are deciding to get on that ladder. Waiting until we reach the manager level might be too late. Not only have we managed to climb the ladder with less support and equity with our male or white female peers, but the exhaustion and frustration may encourage us to opt out from continuing to the next rung. In the same report, 59 percent of Black women that responded to the survey said they had never had an informal interaction with a senior leader. Sponsoring early and often can help change this statistic so that women of color can see true investment and support of their career goals.

SUMMARY

This manifesto is designed to make inclusive sponsorship easier to understand for executives and create a common foundation for how a sponsor should advocate for their protégés. These four core principles—believing in potential, being generous, taking risks, and sponsoring diverse talent—are not meant to be sweeping declarations of who you are as a sponsor. These principles ground us as leaders on how we should model the way for inclusive sponsorship and connect us to our commitment of paying it forward and investing in others. If we agree to use this Sponsorship Manifesto, or to craft our own, to guide our behavior, we will make sponsorship the true mechanism to propel women of color into senior leadership.

7

THE FIVE C'S OF A
GREAT CAREER SPONSOR

I spent a lot of time over the past two years speaking with women at all stages of their careers about the specific characteristics that make a great sponsor. Each one reflected on her own experiences with sponsorship from the early days in her career when she was given opportunities for stretch assignments all the way to her sponsor putting her name up for promotions. Certainly, there were common themes across all of these unique and compelling stories. Every time a person recounted a story about her sponsor taking action on her behalf, her demeanor changed in a positive way. Her face lit up. You could see the energy flowing through her body like electricity as if something had just been sparked or ignited inside of her. There was a sense of deep gratitude for the experience and a desire to pay it forward to others in her network. In fact, some of the women's sponsors inspired them so deeply that they decided to make sponsorship and advocacy a key part of who they were as leaders. Several women described their sponsorship experience as being pivotal and transformational. Sponsorship came at a time when they did not believe in themselves, but their sponsor saw something different about them that they had not seen before. Their sponsors spoke up within their peer group and promoted their protégés' brands in a direct and fervent way. They were unafraid to open their networking circle for the benefit of their protégés as well. There was also an intrinsic value felt in being a sponsor. Viewing a sponsor as a servant leader was also interwoven throughout each of these stories. After more than thirty interviews, it became clear that there are common, key traits to being an exceptional sponsor and advocate for rising leaders. I have distilled these traits down to five core characteristics fundamental to excelling as a sponsor. I call these the "Five C's of a Great Career Sponsor." As your organization begins to look internally for talent ready to become a sponsor and help develop the pipeline for the future, consider these traits not only as foundational but essential. Additionally, if you are actively seeking sponsorship, evaluating potential sponsors against these five traits will help you determine the right person to be your advocate.

COURAGEOUS

If you asked ten people at random how they would define *courage*, you may get ten completely different answers. To me, courage is all about taking risks in your life, even when you feel fearful or uncertain. For example, public speaking has always been a source of fear for me, even after having given presentations at large events—but I knew that it was an important way to develop my personal brand. Forcing myself to conquer this fear by taking baby steps helped me tremendously in stepping into my courage. Regardless of what definition you prefer, courage is one of the traits that any great sponsor should have. I frequently think back to the best sponsorship relationships I have cultivated over my career, and each of those sponsors at their core was both courageous and bold in their support of me. Courage showed up in many different forms. I recall a time when a sponsor of mine put me up for a promotion to my first executive role. The organization I worked for had a culture of meritocracy, but underneath the surface, it always came down to who could vouch for your knowledge, skills, and abilities to get to the next level. I spent the previous six months doing my homework and ensuring that my performance was stellar. In each of my previous annual reviews, I was rated at "exceeds expectations" and even in some instances scored exceptional in a variety of areas. I lined up my supporters, colleagues within the organization who could also vouch for my collaboration skills and the quality of my work product. I built my brand internally and was starting to develop an external brand within the healthcare industry as a strategist. The business case for my promotion was rock solid. Even with all this support, my sponsor still had to gain approval for the promotion with the higher-ups in the company. She also had to face the fact that the organization had put a general moratorium on promotions, given financial performance and a redesign of the organization that had just started months before. But she believed in my potential. She continued to push through the promotion, fight for a substantial pay increase for me, and approach the CEO for final signoff. It would have been easier and less risky for her to say, "Jhaymee, you've done a great job, but perhaps we should wait on your promotion until we are in a better spot as a company." Who knows how long that would have taken? It could have been several weeks, several months, or even years. But instead, she decided to use her political capital with the CEO to ensure that I was valued and celebrated for the work I'd done. She definitely had a sense of fear about the conversation. I am sure it was abnormal for her to go directly to the CEO with these types of requests—to promote a junior executive at the time. Knowing what she knew about the state of our company, I am certain that she was worried about how this request would be perceived as a reflection of her stewardship as a senior executive. Ultimately, she presented the case, and I was promoted to assistant vice president, with a 25 percent increase in my pay. This is what it means for a sponsor to be courageous.

We all know that courage comes in many different forms. In the workplace, it could be in asking for that promotion you deserve or standing your ground against the corporate bully who is treating you poorly because of your race, sexual orientation, or religion. It also can be in voicing your opinion in a room full of colleagues that don't believe in your position on a specific topic. In sponsorship, it means leveraging your brand to accelerate the brand of your protégé. As a sponsor, it means accepting the fact that you are in a position of not only power but also privilege. Your protégé is trusting you to help them achieve their career goals because you have achieved success in your career, and others within your organization see you as a leader who can develop talented individuals and help them grow. You must have courage as well as trust in your protégé that they will rise to the challenge and step into their potential as well. Without courage and trust together, your ability to be effective in sponsoring others will be greatly diminished.

One of the most important questions asked on the topic of courage is, How do you find courageous sponsors? What do they do that is different from or better than leaders that lack this trait? Have you ever been in the team meeting where you have observed leaders standing up for their colleagues' opinions and ideas? Have you ever been in discussions with your leadership team about whom to give a very challenging client relationship to, and one of your peers mentions a name in a way that makes you think they'd worked together for a long time? You may also have seen colleagues that aren't afraid to offer their opinions. They are unencumbered in advocating for their point of view and have a perspective on life, where they are unafraid to speak their mind. I have witnessed in my career executives who will go to bat for employees who may not have all the requisite experience, yet they will support that employee to the end, constantly finding ways to give them exposure and airtime with their leadership.

COMMITTED

Accountability In the workplace has been a growing topic in leadership over the last couple of years. The notion of executives holding themselves accountable, not only for business results but also for the development of their people, continues to be at the forefront of what excellence in management should be. In sponsorship, accountability shows itself as your commitment to supporting the growth and development of your protégé. I was driving home one day, speaking with a senior female executive who was recounting an experience that she had with a failed sponsorship relationship. She talked about how she advocated for the promotion of a teammate, a rising, high potential Black man, and unfortunately this person was not selected for the job she had nominated him for. Of course, her protégé was disappointed and upset at the outcome. Shockingly, she told me that his reaction to the news gave her pause in wanting to support other opportunities for him in the future. He felt that he was deserving of the role and believed that he had been passed over for it because of institutionalized racism bubbling under the surface in the organization. For him, his energy in wanting to be nominated for a future role started to diminish. He felt dejected and demoralized and was doubting his ability to ever be promoted within the organization. I am certain that there was more to this story, but the story planted a question in my mind about why she was so quick to remove her advocacy of her protégé simply because he was unhappy that he didn't get the job. It didn't feel to me that she was very committed to try again. This would have been the perfect opportunity for her to give him some coaching. She could step deeper into her leadership to uncover the *why* behind his feelings but also provide a bit of mentorship and paint a picture for him about how he could position himself even better for opportunities like this going forward. This wasn't the first time I had heard a story like this. A sponsor advocates for an employee, many times an employee of color, and if the result isn't positive, the sponsor retreats and doesn't attempt to advocate for that employee in other areas. This is not only upsetting but is also counterproductive to the core of what it means to be a sponsor.

If I have agreed to be a sponsor for you, I will continue my advocacy of your career growth regardless of the outcome. I have had many stories of, and attempts at, sponsoring protégés that didn't pan out. Either the protégé wasn't selected for the job or speaking engagement, or it simply wasn't the right time for the protégé to make a career move. But those doors closing simply lit a fire within me to try again and again. Eventually, there will be more successes than failures on your sponsorship journey. The persistence and perseverance of a sponsor in helping you reach your career goals are critical traits to consider in finding a great sponsor. Additionally, I have a sense of accountability to make continued attempts at helping my protégé succeed. Giving up simply because the outcome was not what I expected or because my protégé wasn't successful in achieving their goal is very shortsighted. My relationships with my protégés are long term and enduring. My personal accountability to identify and support opportunities for their next career steps is very high. Developing talent is hard work, and many doors will close before one opens. Calling yourself a sponsor means being willing to knock on those doors and continuing your advocacy, even if the result is not ideal. Your commitment to your protégé's success is what they will remember and what you'll be remembered for.

CONNECTED

Back in 2009, I joined a professional women's organization called 85 Broads, now known as Ellevate. I attended an event on networking and met a prolific author named Kelly Hoey, who had just published a book about how she leveraged networking in her career. I immediately bought a copy because networking was something that gave me great anxiety. As an early careerist at the time, I viewed networking as something that was unfamiliar, uncomfortable, and at times sleazy. I always felt awkward chatting with people I didn't know with an obscure goal to get their business card and it magically turning into a new opportunity for me. Her book *Build Your Dream Network: Forging Powerful Relationships in a Hyper Connected World* was a game changer for me. It completely reframed in my mind the purpose of networking, but more importantly, what the power that building a great network can do for you personally and professionally. I have given this book to many protégés over the last ten years. Kelly writes eloquently about accessing your network and understanding the strength and potential gaps in it. Are there people in your network who have their own networks? Are those networks broad (with many people) or are they deep (fewer people but deeper relationships)? Up until this point, I had never thought of my network in that way. My quick assessment was that my network was not intentional and that I hadn't done the work to understand who was even in my network. As I became more senior in my career, I joined many more professional organizations to learn more about new industries and to connect with peers and other senior leaders to build relationships. As these relationships developed, I found that these new connections led to additional introductions, which then led to greater opportunities for my visibility within my industry. My first-ever speaking engagement resulted from a connection I made at a conference reception after I was introduced to a business owner that was looking for a leader to do a presentation on strategy and project management. I started thinking about how blind I was to the fact that new connections have their own connections. The more genuine relationships you develop, the greater the opportunity of meeting future advocates for your brand and your career.

Networking has a multiplier effect on being able to find sponsors. Think of networking as a more direct approach to finding executives that will understand your gifts, your brand, and your potential. Going one step further, having people in your network who are well connected and have their own relationships in industries or organizations that are interesting to you creates a higher probability of finding additional sponsors for yourself. When people know your skills and expertise and have a personal connection with you, they will tell their networks about you. In a lot of ways, your network serves as your brand ambassador. Essentially, sponsors are brand ambassadors specifically for you. I liken this to having a fabulous experience at a restaurant. If you have a wonderful meal, you jump at the opportunity to tell your family and friends about your experience in the hopes that they will also enjoy it. It is certainly free marketing for the restaurant when people are sharing their experience by word of mouth. Similarly, sponsors are sharing by word of mouth your future potential within their circles. Having sponsors and advocates who are well connected gives you broader exposure beyond your role, your organization, and industry. Seeking out executives that have attractive professional brands and believe in your potential enables you to have the agility and flexibility to pivot in your career when you need to and reduces the risk of your being limited in your career trajectory.

CANDID

One of the traits of a great sponsor that does not get as much attention as, but is equally (if not more) important to, other traits is candidness. Candidness is the ability of a sponsor to not sugarcoat their protégés' readiness for sponsorship. Think about the last time you received feedback from either a boss, colleague, your partner or spouse, or a friend. When you received that feedback, did you feel that it was delivered in an authentic way, and did you feel that the person delivering that feedback was being truthful about their observations or perceptions about you? When it comes to sponsorship, it is increasingly important to get direct, actionable, and timely feedback about your ability to be sponsored. This is one of the hardest coaching tips I give to potential protégés, particularly when they reach out about finding a sponsor. When I launched my initiative in early 2020, I was flooded by LinkedIn messages and emails from people in my direct or extended network. They were excited about this focus I had on expanding access for sponsorship. Immediately, many asked, "Will you be my sponsor?," or, "How can you help me gain sponsorship?" If you conducted a survey of executive men and women, they would probably tell you that these are often questions they receive as well. Here's the thing. Before you ask for sponsorship, you must do the work to be ready to receive said sponsorship. For example, I once had a sponsor, a Caucasian female senior vice president, sit me down and talk to me, real talk, about how to navigate the organization I was working for. She was very upfront. I was the type of person that at the end of the workday would go directly home, throw off my work clothes, and unwind with a glass of wine in front of the television, watching one of my favorite episodes of *The Real Housewives* (I still do that to this day). I was so exhausted by the end of the day that I skipped out on team-building events, happy hours, or opportunities to grab dinner with the leader on my team. My sponsor was very transparent with me, saying that those opportunities were hidden gems to find sponsors and for my colleagues to get to know me better. She even said that by not attending those sorts of events, I was missing out on differentiating myself from my peers. She said that doing great work in the office was not enough. I had to do something more. I had to engage socially to round out my ability to develop relationships. Now, my personality lends itself well to engaging socially. I'm naturally an extrovert and get energy from being around other people. Generally, I can find ways to connect with people on a variety of topics—sports, current events, or the latest Michelin star restaurant I have visited. However, I sometimes struggle with regulating my energy at work, especially if I have spent the last eight hours dealing with micro aggressions in the workplace and all I want to do is go home to my family. In fact, many of my Black and Brown colleagues have experienced the same problem. While she listened to me describing these struggles, she maintained that it was imperative for me to find an authentic way to show up. If I had asked another colleague for feedback on this issue, they might have said to just focus on doing great work, instead of giving me candid feedback that would up my game even further. This was a common thread through all of comments of the twenty-plus women and men I spoke to as a part of writing this book—they had someone, usually a sponsor, who had that real-talk conversation with them, even if the messages were difficult to hear. Sometimes the news was good, that is, that someone was willing to be a sponsor for them, and they then derived a plan for how that sponsorship would play out. Sometimes the news was that they were not sponsor-ready and that they needed to spend more time focusing on the tangibles and intangibles that would attract sponsors and the organizations. Candidness is a trait that should not be taken for granted when you are identifying the right type of sponsor for you.

CAPITAL

I remember the first time I heard a TED Talk on the topic of sponsorship. I have admired Carla Harris, managing director at Morgan Stanley, for decades. In fact, she was featured on the cover of a magazine, at the time called *Pink*, along with one of my other professional crushes, Mellody Hobson. Since then, I have been enamored by how she built her career and, more importantly, how bold she is on the topic of leadership excellence through sponsorship. Her talk has garnered millions of views and is frequently quoted as a must-watch among business leaders. She discusses the exchange of professional capital and relationship capital to find the right sponsors for you. She was very open and candid about the sponsors in her career who helped her catapult up the corporate ladder and how she is paying it forward by being a sponsor for others. Coincidentally, several of the men and women I interviewed for this book referenced Carla's talk as inspiration for their own sponsorship journeys. There have been many common themes across these discussions, but when I asked each interviewee what sponsorship meant to them, they unequivocally talked about a leader using their personal or political capital for the advancement of their protégé. This goes to the heart of one of the most important leadership traits around influencing others. Capital allows you to do this with greater power and effect than any other leadership trait. We're not talking about money here, although having political and social capital can in many ways be even more powerful than money. This is the type of leader whom others listen to and want to follow. They are masterful in having influence over their peers and higher-ups. When they walk into a room, not only do they have presence, but their viewpoints are listened to and in many ways celebrated. They have also been successful at navigating their careers within the organization. They know very well the political approaches to how to get things done and who to engage to get things done. Most importantly, they have a way of getting what they want. I feel, specifically for women of color, that this is a trait that should not be missed.

Too often I have talked to rising BIPOC female leaders who gravitate toward people who they think have capital. The inconvenient truth is that many organizations still overwhelmingly have opportunities to diversify their leadership, and many of the executives within their companies who have capital are white. They are also overwhelmingly male. Yet, when I talk to women of color like myself and ask whom they have identified as a sponsor, typically they will choose the person that looks like them to be their sponsor. That feels normal and comfortable to us. Sadly, when we go for that promotion or an opportunity that will get us more visibility in the organization, it turns out that the person we identified as a sponsor did not have the power to make that opportunity happen. This is not to say that a rising Black executive should not select another Black executive to be their sponsor. It simply means that understanding organizational politics and power dynamics in the context of diversity within a company is important to creating equitable access to sponsorship.

When I spoke with a Black female executive at Bank of America, she specifically noted her intention to develop relationships with senior white men on a deeper level because she understood the power dynamics at play once you climb the corporate ladder. She noticed that she tended to gravitate toward other Black senior women because she wanted to understand how they were able to achieve their career goals and get promoted. What she uncovered in those conversations was that those same women also thought very intentionally about who should represent them in the room and, given that their leadership team was almost entirely white, she understood that she needed to focus on expanding her viewpoint on who should be her sponsor in the context of race. This approach paid off well for her. She watched quietly in meetings to see which executives had not only developed talent but also had a track record of promoting from within. She found ways to make direct connections with them, either through engaging socially outside of the organization or being caught in the elevator together and discussing her recent achievements.

Leadership circles are also very tightknit by design. Those who make it to the senior executive levels are trusted for their level of maturity and discretion related to matters concerning the business and its people. Senior executives have been able to navigate the politics of the organization and create a followership using business savvy. Executives can also be cliquish and rely on each other's influence to advance business objectives, whether they are about company growth, investment in talent, or divesting a division. In essence, a sponsor at the executive level has built their brand and established key relationships that can be leveraged to persuade the organization's leadership to take a specific course of action. A great sponsor is rich with capital. Not only are they wealthy in this regard, but they are unconditional in exchanging their capital to see their protégé succeed within the organization or outside. Capital has great power that can work very quickly if placed in the right hands. One of my good friends, who works for one of the largest pharmaceutical companies globally, underscored this notion in a brief chat that we had in 2019. A simple phone call from one of her company's vice presidents to the chief operating officer (COO) secured a job for a candidate whom very few people within the organization knew. The person didn't participate in any interview process. Quite frankly, there were concerns from HR about this person's background and ability to be a cultural fit. However, the vice president was a sponsor for this candidate and had a relationship with the COO. The two were in each other's weddings, and very frequently could be seen grabbing drinks after hours at their favorite bar. The VP was well respected in the organization and had a track record of developing talent. Senior leaders also viewed this VP as a rising leader and trusted his expertise when it came to hiring decisions. The candidate's hiring process was streamlined. In a few short days, she had a prominent role within the organization. Sponsors with this type of capital can work quickly and efficiently to promote their proteges. Finding a sponsor willing to use their capital is a prominent way for employees to reach their short- and long-term career goals.

KEY TAKEAWAYS

These five C's are great way to assess potential advocates for your career. As you make a list of leaders in your network who can serve as sponsors for you, evaluate them against each of these five traits. While all traits are components of a great sponsor, I would argue that *courageous* and *capital* are the most important in finding a sponsor to champion your success. I cannot stress enough that a sponsor who is vocal and bold and leads with influential capital will be more successful than sponsors that lack these characteristics. Look at leaders in your organizations who have a track record of growing talent. How would they stack up against these five characteristics? How does your boss or superior measure up to these five characteristics as well? You might find that professionals who you thought were sponsors for you are either very strong or have gaps in these five areas. You should be very selective in who serves as your advocate and sponsor, especially if they lack the courage and capital that would be required to achieve positive results for you.

One common fallacy I have observed in talking with mentees and protégés is the assumption that their boss is their sponsor. If that is not an agreed-upon arrangement, however, then the boss is not a sponsor. Sponsorship is intentional and agreed-upon by both parties. Perhaps your boss could be your sponsor, but I would encourage you to look at these five traits and see if your boss has the makings of a great sponsor. If they do and a sponsorship relationship makes sense for you, explore how your relationship can evolve over time into sponsor-protégé. Additionally, this is a great opportunity for professionals that have a lot of mentors in their network to evaluate them against these traits and determine how to convert a mentor to a great sponsor. If you are a woman of color, think about how you can approach your sponsorship network from a diversity lens. Ensure that, as you assess who should sponsor you, you are aware of the sphere of influence within your company, and be strategic about including sponsors in your network who have the power and influence that you need.

Given the talent challenges that many organizations face coupled with increasing desires for more diverse leadership teams, these five traits are also a great assessment for the executives and leaders within your company. If you are with a company that is considering developing a formal sponsorship program, I would caution against selecting participants simply based on title. Using these five traits as evaluation criteria to select sponsor participants is key. These traits can also be helpful if you are considering sponsorship as a leadership competency that the executives in your organization will be held accountable to. These characteristics are also a smart way to positively reinforce the behaviors that you want modeled by leaders across the company. It is important to define what great sponsorship should look and feel like, and these five C's are a perfect foundation to create common language around expectations of sponsorship for your executives. Finally, great sponsors also put a premium on inclusivity. Go further than just encouraging your executives to think about sponsoring diverse proteges. Demand and hold your leadership accountable for sponsoring an employee that looks different from them.

8

SPONSOR READINESS
FOR WOMEN OF COLOR

Since there is a variety of articles, blog posts, and books written about sponsor readiness, key questions you might have are: "How does sponsor readiness look different for women of color? Do women of color need to prepare in a different way to attract and retain sponsors? The answer to both of these questions, in my opinion, is yes. Attracting sponsors in a large way is predicated on how others perceive you. Sure, it is important to layer that perception with tangible facts about your performance. However, sponsorship is all about developing relationships. It is driven by human emotion and interaction. For those of you that have worked in the corporate world, you know that how someone perceives you can very well be their reality about who you are as a person.

The challenging part for women of color is that these perceptions can commonly be clouded by bias, and not just gender bias but also racial bias. Let me give you an example of how this might play out. A few years ago, I took one of my mentees, Vanessa, for our standard quarterly lunch. We had both been looking forward to connecting as it had been some time since our last meeting due to schedule conflicts. We sat down at one of our favorite restaurants in Charlotte and began chatting about the projects we were working on. She shared that she was struggling to connect with one of her bosses, a white female in her early fifties. Her boss, let's call her Diane, had all of the makings of a great sponsor. She was well known in her organization for developing talent and personally played a role in getting three rising female leaders promotions to vice president. She was warm and engaging and seemed to take a genuine interest in the people that worked for her. Previously, I had discussed with my mentee the importance of engaging socially with her colleagues as a way to bilaterally develop relationships and begin connecting with people on a different level. Vanessa had invested a lot of time in participating in team-building activities and afterwork happy hours to break out of her shell and feel comfortable conversing with her team outside of work. She started to gain momentum with Diane in particular, and they started to get to know each other on a more personal level by swapping stories about how they grew up and the people that influenced them the most in their lives. Vanessa felt that they had started to develop a rapport, and in the back of her mind she was thinking of approaching Diane to be her mentor. Her ultimate goal was to learn from Diane in the mentoring relationship, and as she continued performing at work, would eventually ask Diane to be her sponsor. One day at work, Vanessa overheard a few team members talking about a concert that Diane invited them to as a way to relate to them differently. Vanessa was a little perplexed because she hadn't been approached by Diane to attend this concert.

At their next one-on-one meeting, Vanessa decided to be brave and ask Diane about the concert. Vanessa told Diane, "I heard that some of the team is going with you to this concert, and if there is an open spot, I would love to also attend." Admittedly, Vanessa felt sheepish about asking and perhaps, in a way, invited herself to attend by bringing it up. Diane looked confused and responded, "Oh I didn't ask you to attend the concert because it's Kenny Chesney, and I didn't think you'd want to go." Vanessa likewise looked confused and asked Diane, "Why wouldn't I want to go to the concert? It seems like a lot of fun." Diane responded, "Well it's country music and I didn't think that was your type of *thang*." I remember sitting across from Vanessa as she was telling this story, almost choking on my salad and sheer shock. Not only was Diane not being inclusive toward Vanessa but then on top of that assumed that she didn't like country music simply because of the way she looked. By the way, Vanessa is a Black woman from South Carolina who absolutely enjoys country music along with other genres including rap, R&B, and grunge. Again, this potential sponsor assumed something about Vanessa based on perception and essentially closed the door to a potential sponsoring relationship. This is simply one story of many where racial bias could come into play if you let it. As leaders, it becomes critical for you to check your biases at the door and tap further into your curiosity.

On the part of the protégé, especially if you are a woman of color, sponsor readiness means doing the work on yourself personally and professionally to be prepared for someone to invest their time and talent to you. You must have the clarity and conviction about what you want in your career and be able to communicate that in an authentic way to others. I have distilled what sponsor readiness should mean for women of color into four primary areas: investing heavily into networking, accelerating your brand, managing stress, and gaining visibility. Doing these four things exceptionally well will position you to find the right sponsors, who will catapult you forward. Notice that "performing well" was not one of the four areas I highlighted. Here's why. First of all, doing great work has been table stakes for BIPOC women for as long as I have known. I remember sitting at the kitchen table with my mother at age ten and her sharing the biggest lesson she'd learned in her life. She turned to me one morning over breakfast as I was getting ready for school and said, "You will have to work twice as hard to get half as far." She wasn't saying that simply because I was Black. She said it because I am Black and female. Little did I know how true this lesson would be throughout my life. Reemphasizing the need to do great work is insulting to women of color across corporate America. Yes, we know all about having to perform well and have been overperforming for decades. So let's put this piece of the puzzle to the side and accept this as a foundational fact. I would rather focus on the other elements of sponsor readiness that I think will be even more impactful to finding sponsors. Future sponsors, take note. More than likely, if your protégé is a woman of color, she *is* doing the work. What she needs from you is your candid guidance about the quality of her performance and how you can be supportive of her journey for sponsor readiness so that she can shine even brighter.

INVEST HEAVILY IN NETWORKING

Networking is one of the primary ways that you can de-risk the probability of getting a sponsor. The ups and downs of the global economy in 2020 and 2021 are proof of this. You are never in a down economy when you have the right network in place to assist you in either a job search or another professional opportunity. I remember a former boss of mine, and not a good boss, who was critical of the time I had invested in meeting new people. In fact, she once told me directly, "I think you network too much." In my mind, that meant I was doing it right. We have all heard the age-old saying "It's not *what* you know, it's *who* you know." We also know that organizations have harped on the fact that they can't find talented diverse professionals within their companies. You have to get out there. You have to find ways for executives and leaders to find you if for no other reason than to eliminate the excuse that you don't exist. Now, I understand that in general for women of color, the idea of networking seems like an overwhelming and daunting task. As I've said before in this book, earlier in my career I thought that networking was extremely superficial and not comfortable for me at all. It took years of practice to get to the point where I'm feeling comfortable in my own skin at networking events. There are still times when it feels awkward, but I push myself to take small steps anytime I feel uneasy about networking. For example, if you are introverted, or perhaps the stress that schmoozing adds to a social event makes your stomach flip, there are other ways to have the same if not better impact in establishing new relationships with people in your industry. Social media has made it much easier for professionals to network. One of my favorite platforms for networking is LinkedIn. It's not a perfect solution, but it certainly allows you to directly connect with people you find interesting or companies you are interested in learning more about in a safer environment. Simply liking a person's post or article, or even commenting on something someone in your network has shared can establish an instant connection. The same can be said for other mediums like Twitter or Instagram, and it can also be a lot of fun to engage in a digital way.

As I mentioned before, networking does take time, but it is well worth your energy. You don't have to spend hours and hours of your time, but you do have to be strategic in figuring out what networking activities will have maximum impact for you in finding sponsors. One that I highly recommend is joining a professional association. It could be industry specific, or it could be a group of likeminded executive women looking to connect and have fellowship, like Chief or, C200, or the Women Business Leaders in the Healthcare Industry (WBL). Foundations have even been established to create scholarships for women to develop themselves and become sponsor-ready. The Carol Emmott fellowship is a prominent program that sponsors twenty women each year to fully develop themselves into executives in the healthcare industry. Some of my most treasured sponsors have come from membership organizations that I joined mid-career and have connected with on a variety of topics—be it diversity and inclusion or health equity or leadership excellence. Find a community that will put you in the orbit of leaders you admire and believe could be a sponsor for you.

Conversely, if you are a sponsor, there are several ways you can help your protégé invest in their network. More than likely, you have amassed high-profile relationships with executives within either your company or your discipline. A low-risk high-impact action would be to invite your protégé into your networking circle and make some strategic introductions for her. A great sponsor would know what your protégés' goals are, and you can match your protégé with people in your network who will give her additional perspectives. If you happen to work directly with your protégé, consider bringing her into some of your senior-level exclusive meetings. This will not only give her visibility with your peers and superiors, but it will also deepen your relationship with her and build trust that you are genuinely interested in helping her advance. Remember, being a sponsor means taking action, and demonstrating your commitment to taking action is the core of inclusive sponsorship.

ACCELERATE YOUR BRAND

I have never been a marketer professionally, but I will tell you that branding is essential to distinguishing yourself from others. Think of the brands and companies you enjoy most; they have done a masterful job at connecting the value of their products to your emotions. There is a sense of bonding in the relationship because the brand has established a connection and trust with you that you will get high quality each and every time you purchase their product. You want that same relationship with your sponsor. Establishing your brand is a direct route in gaining sponsorship for your career. When a sponsor believes in your brand, they will become your brand ambassador and will champion you effortlessly and unconditionally. Branding gives you visibility as well. As a woman of color, I have benefited from establishing my brand and allowing it to find opportunities for me. My position as a thought leader on gender equality, diversity in healthcare, and leadership has opened opportunities for me to offer my point of view at well-known entities such as *Modern Healthcare*, Ellevate, and The Lily. Think about what thought-leadership circles you belong to and where you might be able to add value. Offer to coauthor an article with your sponsor on your leadership journey or to be interviewed for a book your colleague is writing about women in leadership. You could even write a personal memoir or a book on your ideas for the future of leadership. You have a unique perspective, and your story deserves to be heard.

How should you approach accelerating your brand? It's simple. Take a course. I was introduced to Stephen A. Hart, an exceptional expert in personal brand development, as part of a writer's retreat that I took from Minda Harts. Yes, *that* Minda Harts, the amazing author of *The Memo* and *Right Within*, and also a friend and mentor. Stephen's boot camp, Brand You Academy, was life changing for me. It went beyond thinking about the content that I wanted to be known for and focused on my visual identity. How was I showing up aesthetically on my website? What are my brand colors? What topography did I want associated with who I am? All of these were questions I explored over the course of twelve weeks. It made me think about the importance of establishing connections based on the consistency and clarity of my visual brand.

Also, I wanted to dig into the conversations I wanted to have publicly about the topics that I was most passionate about. When you have a brand as a thought leader, people with the same interests and passions as you will want to continue the conversation. You will be sought out for your knowledge as well as your uniqueness in your space. Continuing on the theme of taking classes to accelerate my brand, I signed up for a course with the Carol Cox Thought Leadership Academy to hone my presentation skills. My goal was to create a signature talk on this very topic around sponsorship, having seen a colleague of mine at a former company do this and monetize it for herself. She leveraged her signature talk as her platform and used it with a variety of clients and companies that were interested in hearing her speak. It gave her visibility and credibility and accelerated her brand outside of our company. She was receiving requests to make presentations right and left, and she flourished beyond her current professional role.

Taking classes on your visual identity and thought leadership are great ways to extend your brand, but you should also engage in the conversation yourself. Once you have carefully crafted your message and have thought through the points you want to make, don't be afraid to get on stage and share your ideas more broadly. There is a shortage of women of color in particular who have established themselves as thought leaders. Yet there is a hunger for greater diversity in the speakers circle. Event planners are looking for Black, Latina, Asian, and Native women to have their opportunity on the in-person or virtual stage. Too many events have the dreaded "manel," panel discussions where all participants are male. I am very aware of this phenomenon, as I have had discussions with event planners about being thoughtful and strategic with people participating at these events. This is an area where people are looking for you. If you are ready and have a message, the world is your oyster. Take advantage of speaking opportunities at conferences, on podcasts, and in webinars. These are tried-and-true ways of getting your name and your brand out to a larger audience. I am specifically a fan of podcasts. These are quick yet impactful ways to demonstrate your expertise, and for those of you afraid of public speaking, this is a low-risk opportunity. Podcast episodes are easily shareable on your personal website or on social media. Often, speaking on podcasts gives you opportunities to speak at even more prestigious engagements. When you can share your authentic voice, people connect with you in ways that wouldn't be available at the office.

As a sponsor, you play a key role in accelerating your protégés' brand. Your influence and political capital carries weight with those in your network and your peers at your company as well. Because of this, your protégés look to you to amplify their message as a strong advocate. It is a precious component of your servant leadership and one that should not be taken lightly. Being a sponsor is a role of accountability and responsibility. If you are unwilling to be your protégé's advocate and promote their brand, you should reconsider whether you are the right sponsor for them. One way to equip yourself as a strong sponsor is to ask your protégés to provide you with a sheet of talking points of their accomplishments and goals. This is more than just a résumé. These are bullet points that give the sponsor a quick picture into the type of projects protégés are leading, with quantifiable metrics of success. Having just a few bullet points in your back pocket will allow you to quickly share with your connections why this person is worthy of your sponsorship. If your protégé is a board candidate, ask for their board bio, which is a narrative of their most salient accomplishments that can also be easily shared with others. Most importantly, be sure that you understand your protégé's career goals and be thoughtful about sharing those goals within your network.

MANAGE STRESS LEVELS

Most people wouldn't naturally see the connection between managing their stress level and becoming sponsor-ready. The higher up you go in an organization, the more responsibility you have, which can lead to stressful situations. As an executive, you are entrusted with proprietary information about your company and are expected to hold this information in confidence and with discretion. More than likely at this level, you are also a people leader and are dealing with a variety of situations that the people you lead experience day to day. As you continue developing yourself as a leader, You will be expected to manage your stress and understand the triggers that may cause you to tap into your negative behaviors. Without managing your stress, your performance could be negatively impacted, and others may see you as erratic and unable to handle the pressure of being a leader. Generally speaking, people gravitate to leaders who are able to remain calm under pressure, find solutions, and lead their teams through challenging situations in a positive spirit. You will attract sponsors that see you as a levelheaded executive and feel comfortable with you. This is why stress management is so essential to your sponsor readiness.

Combined with stress management is prioritizing your mental wellness. Given our exposure to micro aggressions on a daily basis, this becomes even more important for women of color. You will show up as an effective leader when you take time for yourself to recharge. One of my favorite quotes comes from Oprah Winfrey; it's about not being able to pour from an empty cup. When you are sapped of energy, you are that empty cup. This takes me back to the story I shared with you about being bullied by a former boss. Every day when I arrived at work I felt like an empty cup. Being able to show up for my team was a constant struggle. Knowing that I was the only person of color on her team having this experience saddened me and was emotionally draining. One thing I decided to do, a best practice I carried into the next chapter of my career, is what I call Wellness Wednesdays. The idea actually came years prior when I worked for a boss that used to regularly take a mental wellness day. It was one day a month, when he would turn off his cell phone and all email communication and focus on doing something purely for himself. For him, this involved going to the movies or visiting his beach house in Delaware. The rule is that you should do whatever brings you joy on that day. Only you can define that for yourself. For me, I designated Wednesday as my mental wellness day. I look forward to it every month. I block it on my calendar as a private event in Outlook, and I take that day simply to recharge myself. Sometimes I exercise on my Peloton bike. Other days I take a trip to the spa. And other days I curl up with a nice book next to my fireplace and read. By the way, my Wellness Wednesday is not only off limits to my work team, but also off limits to my husband. He knows that this day is for me and makes sure I have complete solitude and silence. Think about other ways that will help you manage your stress, and don't buy into the stigma about needing help. Therapy is a healthy practice that I highly encourage as it gives you a safe space and an objective opinion on how you can understand your triggers and find solutions.

Another thing I decided to do as I was focusing on my wellness practice was to get an executive and a life coach. At the time, I needed both in my life. I was so stressed at work that I would bring it all home. Because I was too stressed at work, I was not able to be my high-performing self with my team. It was a vicious cycle that seemed never-ending. Coincidentally, my executive coach, Dr. Sharon Melnick, had written a book about how to lead through stress. Her book, *Success under Stress*, gave me several tips and tricks on how to navigate stressful situations and be in my power. For so long, I had let stress overtake me, and I felt completely out of control in my destiny. Her book showed me how to focus on the things within my control and how to communicate in a way that taps into my power and influence.[1] Understanding what I wanted long-term in my career and translating my goals into "What's in it for them" allowed me to direct my superiors and sponsors to jump in and assist me. I consider my executive and life coaches to be part of my personal board of directors, which is another name for my success team. There's this theme of psychological safety that I've mentioned several times in this book, and both give me that space to be completely in my power while exploring how I can be a better version of myself. You don't have to only get a coach when you're in a crisis. Coaches can help you think through what's next for you in your career and even give you guidance on how to approach gaining sponsors. Coaches are also great at helping you solve problems by giving you frameworks to use to break down problems and providing you the tools to solve them.

Yes, as a sponsor, you have a role to play in helping your protégés manage stress. If your protégé is a woman of color, be the reliable safe space that they can come to by being an active listener. You may not always be able to truly understand their experience but listening with empathy goes a long way to strengthening the sponsorship relationship. Educate yourself on the lived experiences of women of color. Read the studies and dig into the data. Consider having discussions with your protégé about what you've learned, and ask them how you can be the best sponsor for them. Encourage your peers to do the same with their protégés. Probably the most important way you can show up as a great sponsor is to challenge the negative perceptions that your colleagues may have about your protégé. One of the biggest pain points I have around performance evaluations is the language used for people of color that overtly and covertly places the person in a negative light. Whether it's that a Black woman is too aggressive, or a Latina is not a team player, don't be afraid to nudge and dig a little deeper and asked for specifics. If your protégé reports to you, ask for specific examples and behaviors that they displayed that led to a certain comment or rating. If there is a perception that she is not a cultural fit for the team, ask the team to define what that means. Come equipped with the data that allows you to serve as her advocate.

GET RECOGNIZED FOR YOUR WORK

How often do women of color get recognized for their contributions in the workplace? The data suggests the frequency is very low. In fact, women of color feel that others get credit for the work that we do.[2] We continue to be underrepresented when it comes to industry or national awards or even within our own organizations. The downside to this is that if we aren't getting recognized for our work and our accomplishments do not have visibility, and thus our access to sponsors becomes diminished. I also believe that women of color are commonly told that receiving recognition for our accomplishments is somehow dirty. Our work has to be in the broader context of the team. If we individually shine bright, we are seen as being boastful. So we keep our heads down, do great work, and miss out on opportunities to showcase our work products. I am here to say, don't believe the hype. In the words of Rihanna, "Shine bright like a diamond!" Believe me, I understand the hesitance in wanting to receive recognition for your work. There are countless stories from women in my network where recognition backfired. One hundred percent of these stories were from women of color. One of my colleagues at a large pharmaceutical company was unjustly let go because she received an industry award that a white male in her organization felt deserved it more. My being bullied in the workplace arose from being selected for a national industry Top 40 list that circulated within my team and triggered my former boss. The moment women of color begin to receive recognition for their work, a target is placed on her back. Fear begins to settle in. If I get an award for efforts I led, who in my organization will have a problem with it? Will my job be at risk if someone nominates me for an industry recognition? I get it. It can be very dangerous and scary to think about. It is amazing how we are conditioned to immediately think about the negative aspect of recognition. It's almost a knee-jerk reaction. But here's the thing. If you never get recognized for your work, no one will know who you are. No one can find you. If no one sees your work as being worthy, how can sponsors want to support you? It is not sinful to receive credit for your work, and it is certainly not vain or conceited to receive an award for your accomplishments. Stop the negative talk to yourself about this. We need to change our perspective.

The key to being recognized for your work is to make it seem as though it is someone else's idea. I am sure you are familiar with subliminal advertising. Planting the seed by sharing the outcomes of your project and your role in leading that project can spark interest from others in spotlighting you. Some people call this an elevator speech. I call it a strategic nudge. You are sharing information and insights about the work you know intimately about. You have a unique perspective and a point of view that no one else has because you led the work. But even if you plant the seed, sometimes you have to help it grow. The ugly truth is that you can plant lots of seeds and they never grow. You can continue to campaign and share your successes with others, but they are not inspired to take action and recognize you for your efforts. In this case, don't be afraid to self-nominate. If there is an industry award that you think you are qualified for, nominator yourself if they accept nominations. Of course, this can be tricky if you work in a cultural environment that is political about awards and recognition. You have to be savvy to know when to ask for permission and when to ask for forgiveness. If self-nomination isn't an option, ask for someone to nominate you. Again, there is nothing wrong with approaching your sponsor and asking him or her to nominate you for recognition. A great sponsor will jump at the chance to support your nomination. This is a wonderful way to engage peer sponsors, a topic to be discussed in another chapter. Peer sponsors tend to be closer to understanding your work and can speak very intelligently about the impact you've made because they work more directly with you.

So why am I so focused on awards and recognition as a way of gaining sponsorship? First, awards and recognition are direct ways to get your name publicly in the orbit of high-impact and influential leaders. You can argue about the validity of industry awards and how important they are for your career. At the end of the day, seeing your name on an industry list also accelerates your brand and ways for people to find you. You are probably picking up on this common theme about people finding you. This is key. There is a halo effect that comes from receiving an award that is well known and respected. Human nature suggests that if other people think you are worthy, then you must be worthy. If it is a well-respected award, you have been through the due diligence and the rigor to receive it. And as I've said before, there is a severe lack of recognition for women of color across all industries. So if you do receive an award, it will be memorable to others. I am not suggesting that your goal in your career should be to amass every single award out there. However, I do think being strategic about what your end game is and how awards and recognition fit into that will help you immensely on your journey to sponsorship.

If you are a sponsor, this is where you can thrive. First and foremost, you are probably well aware of your industry's awards and recognition programs and processes and, specifically, which awards are worthy of nomination. Be generous here. Find ways to nominate your protégés for industry awards. If your protégé is earlier in their career, there are many "under 40" and "emerging leader" lists that can be a boost for them. In recent years, awards for diverse leaders have become more popular than ever. This is also a good way to recognize your protégés that are women of color. I would stress not to focus on these types of awards as the only recognition that you nominate your protégés for. Some of the most prominent and prestigious awards do not have a diversity component, but they tend to carry a lot of weight in how they are viewed and respected within your industry. Consider nominating a woman of color for these types of awards to extend greater credibility to their accomplishments. Awards aren't the only thing you can nominate your protégés for. As I mentioned before, a speaking engagement at a conference is another great way for you to support and be a brand ambassador for your protégé. Just one speaking engagement can have a lasting impact on building your protégé's confidence as well as giving them exposures to other potential sponsors as well.

9

CREATING AN INCLUSIVE SPONSORSHIP CULTURE

THE UNCONSCIOUS BIAS OF SPONSORSHIP

I recall talking to someone in my network as I decided to write this book specifically around sponsorship for diverse women. One of the questions he asked me was, How does sponsorship look different for women of color? Aren't the tactics the same? At face value, I'm sure many people are asking the same question. What truly is different about sponsoring a Black woman versus a white woman? Or even, How is it different between genders? I've thought about this in detail, and I reflected on the sponsorship relationships I've had as both a sponsor and a protégé. Here's what I've discovered. Sure, some of the tactics are absolutely similar. I've given the same advice in a lot of ways to women regardless of race. The difference, in my opinion, is the intentionality of the relationship and the experience that a protégé goes through with their sponsor that may differ because of unconscious bias. Remember that when the #MeToo movement started and gained attention, there was an unease around male colleagues having any sort of interaction with their female colleagues. I personally have heard men at work discussing how they don't even want to close the door during meetings for fear that it would be perceived the wrong way. A distance started to grow between men and women at work. Similarly, that same fear has been pervasive in corporate America around race and race relations as a result of the police brutality and murders, particularly among Black males. There was trepidation by white colleagues in wanting to talk to their Black colleagues about their experience at work based on their race. And there probably was a fear of providing feedback to Black colleagues about their performance so as to not offend them and be caught in a situation where they would be reprimanded by their company's HR department. This is real talk. These two fears, based on gender and race, have continued to exacerbate the problem of access to sponsorship for women of color. And it's especially troubling since, unfortunately, the majority of sponsors with influence and power within organizations are white and male. Strong leadership requires courage and intentionality and a willingness to do what's right for employees and what is right for the organization.

As organizational leaders, it's important to realize that in order to encourage a culture of sponsorship, your company must have the right culture for it to flourish. This doesn't happen overnight. Creating a sponsorship culture requires intentionality on the part of senior leadership, and it also requires thoughtfulness about selecting executives to serve as active sponsors for rising diverse talent. In most organizations, sponsors tend to bubble up organically. Usually, a leader that has a strong spike in giving back to others will look within his or her universe for protégés to sponsor. That universe is typically limited in scope and to employees whom the leaders have worked directly with on projects and initiatives. There has to be consensus within your leadership ranks that creating the pipeline of talent is a core responsibility of people managers. It is not enough simply to have competency. It is a core competency if you have responsibility for leading employees.

The other piece to this equation is understanding that there is an inherent unconscious bias of sponsorship. First, sponsors tend to advocate for and support protégés who look like them. They went to the same school. Their families attend the same church. They're in the same social circles. There is something outside of work connecting them together so that they are in each other's orbit. Because of this, sponsors tend to have protégés of the same race, religion, or socioeconomic background. This makes it increasingly difficult to create access to sponsorship for employees from underrepresented minority groups. If there isn't some form of personal connection or commonality between the sponsor and protégé, more than likely there will continue to be issues of sameness. Building on this concept of sameness is the bias that clouds the perceptions of women of color in the workplace specifically. Aside from what we know about perceptions of women from specific racial or ethnic groups, there are often higher expectations placed on women of color regarding their experience, educational pedigree, and workplace performance.

This becomes abundantly apparent during the annual performance review process and during interviews as well. It is one of the key reasons why companies have moved to blind interview procedures, removing the name of candidates and letting their résumé stand on its own. Personally, I have been a participant and observer of annual reviews that have gone sideways for employees of color, especially if the panel of reviewers is not diverse. What tends to happen in the conversation is that a diverse woman who has performed exceptionally well in her work is still being viewed as not ready for a promotion or the next step in her career. She's had years of above-average ratings, and yet there tends to be caution around elevating her to the next level for fear that she will fail in that role. You don't tend to hear these conversations about male employees. In fact, what I've observed is that if a male colleague is not ready for the next step or promotion, leadership swoops in to provide wrap-around executive coaching and development programs to ensure that he succeeds. The same should be put on the table for women of color. As I mentioned in my earlier discussion around courage, this is where a true sponsor has an essential and critical role for their protégés. Speaking up and advocating when you are in the room during these conversations can absolutely change the mindset of your leadership team. Don't allow bias to seep in when evaluating your protégés of color. Be sure, if you have an opinion about your protégé, that you voice your opinion in the moment, not after the meeting has concluded or a few weeks later. You have to take a stand actively right then and there.

What can organizations do to create the best culture for sponsorship? There are six primary ways to build this foundation within your organization. One thing to note that would be a "derailleur" is that senior leadership needs to believe not only that creating a pipeline of diverse talent is their responsibility but also that sponsorship is the mechanism by which diversity can grow and thrive within the company. Without this common belief, senior leaders will opt out if they don't find accountability within themselves to be a solution to this challenge. The truth is you will have leaders that decide not to participate. But you have to have the conviction to push forward with the leaders that get it—who understand and can empathize with having a sponsor in their career and how their sponsors have made a material impact on their journeys. Following are the six things organizations can do.

INCLUSIVE SPONSORSHIP AS A LEADERSHIP COMPETENCY

As an executive talent advisor, I'm always curious about how leadership competencies are defined and what they truly mean for the development of executive leadership. I wanted to find a definition that was clear and concise and got to the root of why it's important. For this, I went to one of the most well-respected associations for human capital development. The Society for Human Resources Management (SHRM) has defined leadership competencies as "leadership skills and behaviors that contribute to superior performance."[1] Seems pretty straightforward, right? I would argue that *inclusive* sponsorship is both a skill and behavior that directly contributes to a company's superior performance. *Full stop.* For managers to see their role as increasing diversity and inclusion, they also have to view it as essential to their daily work. Developing your team so that members can operate at their best has been a competency at management levels for decades. Making inclusive sponsorship a core competency to developing future leaders weaves in accountability. And this should start even before employees become people managers. It should be introduced at all levels in the organization, giving employees more time to practice and model these behaviors. So, what should those behaviors be? Building relationships is chief among them. This behavior has a tangible impact on creating a positive work environment that should be exemplified and directly contributes to improving the psychological safety for diverse employees. Leaders should make the time for relationship development—in fact, I block time in my Outlook calendar so that I can be focused and present with my colleagues. Whether it's going out to lunch or going on a walk during a break, take thirty minutes out of your day to connect with a diverse team member. Find out what they are working on and be genuinely interested in hearing about their accomplishments and successes. It creates a foundation for trust to take root when you swap stories about presentation that you knocked out of the park or empathize with a difficult client and collectively figure out how to move forward with them. And you don't have to wait to be an executive to practice this behavior. Early and mid-careerists should also build muscle memory into developing relationships with colleagues and peers. As a leader, encourage your teammates to schedule time for one-on-one connections with each other, and nudge them to connect with a team member they don't know.

The other behavior that can foster the right environment for inclusive sponsorship is self-education on diversity, equity, and inclusion. If you want to sponsor diverse women, you have to understand their lived experience. Certainly, you can learn more about these experiences by developing relationships with your diverse protégés. But push yourself as a sponsor to go one step further. There is an abundance of information and knowledge, including this book, about the unique challenges of women of color in the workplace. Equip yourself with data, and supplement that data with real-life testimonies from diverse women—and actively listen. Your role is not to debate or offer a counter-opinion to what she has experienced. And while you are not able to fully relate to or appreciate their stories, the simple act of engaging in (and not shying away from) the discussion demonstrates your authentic commitment to inclusive sponsorship. Having this information also allows you to be even bolder in your sponsorship by challenging your superiors and colleagues on perceptions of women of color in your organization. You will have the data and the language to be effective in your advocacy.

MOVE YOUR ORGANIZATION FROM
MENTORSHIP TO INCLUSIVE SPONSORSHIP

There is no shortage of mentorship programs available for high-potential employees. I am certain that your organization has at least one
of those programs in place today. All of these programs have good in-
tentions. Matching employees with senior leaders that can give them
the coaching they need to develop is a wonderful way to increase employee engagement and also build relationships across your company.
Many employees feel enriched that their organization is investing in
them. Additionally, leaders that participate as mentors find intrinsic
value in serving others, and many are flattered by the simple identifi-
cation of them as mentors. However, there are a couple of problems
with launching only mentorship programs, either formal or informal.
First is the so-what factor. An employee participates and gets months
of coaching and exposure to a senior leader, but the unintended
consequence is that, as that program concludes, employees feel be-
wildered about what is next, either for the relationship itself or for
their career. Second, mentorship is a low-risk activity, meaning that
there is no expectation on the part of the mentor beyond simply acting as a coach to the mentee. Relationships conclude, but sometimes
there is an aftereffect of continued relationship development. But
more often than not, there is no true outcome around advancing the
employee in her career. Sponsorship takes a different approach. It is a
higher risk, higher reward behavior. The sponsor has to take action,
and there can be a range of actions that he or she can take. But there
is that thread of accountability in sponsorship that is generally not
present in mentorship. Calling yourself a sponsor without advocating
and acting on behalf of your protégé is simply mentorship in sheep's
clothing. Truly being a sponsor means that there was an action and an
outcome that is tangible and impactful to the protégé. Earlier in the
book, I discussed how specifically women of color are over-mentored
and under-sponsored. Lots of coaching and advice. Not a whole lot
of action happening on the advocacy front. But all is not lost. Truth-
fully, many sponsorship relationships start in mentorship. Think about
it. In mentoring, you meet over a series of activities that are designed

to build relationships with your mentee. Most often, you hear about the tremendous challenges facing her in the workplace and provide your wise counsel on how to navigate those challenges. You have developed trust. You start to get to know each other personally and uncover a lot of commonalities you have. Mentorship quite frankly is a great foundation for sponsorship to arise from. I consider it the first part of a trilogy, the trilogy being the three phases in everyone's career journey. Part 1 is getting the coaching and advice as a rising leader (mentorship). Part 2 is obtaining the advocacy and support needed to advance (sponsorship). Part 3 is paying it back and creating the next generation of leadership. As a company, it is actually quite easy to move your organization from mentorship to inclusive sponsorship. One way to do this is to expand your mentorship program and treat it as part one of a two-part journey between the mentor and the mentee. Treat it as a graduation from mentorship. Once the mentor and mentee have established the relationship, sponsorship becomes an organic and natural extension of it that doesn't feel awkward or forced. Even if you have leaders that are not participating in your company's formal mentorship program, ask them to examine their mentorship relationships that evolved those into sponsorships. Ask them for a list of their high-potential employees, and challenge them to ensure that that slate is diverse. Just imagine if every single executive in your company took one of their mentees and decided to deepen the relationship and transition from being a mentor to a sponsor. It's not a monumental task. It is a bite-sized way for executives to have a direct impact on the lives and careers of an employee they already have a relationship with. Holding executives accountable for inclusive sponsorship also becomes easier when the relationship with their mentee has been formed and nurtured.

TELL STORIES ABOUT INCLUSIVE SPONSORSHIP SUCCESS

Stories are a powerful way to connect us all on an emotional level. Organizations are astute about this. If you're a leader, you've probably received a newsletter about the financial performance of the organization or that big client that your company was able to develop. We celebrate the wins, big and small, as a way to motivate the workforce to do better and be better. I have found that stories related to sponsorship are lacking. It's one of the reasons why in 2020 I started a series called Stories of Sponsorship. True stories of my experience either being sponsored or having sponsored others. When people can see the impact of sponsorship, it becomes inspirational, especially when you break down how easy sponsorship can be. If you want to create an environment of inclusive sponsorship, you have to be willing to not only tell these stories but also celebrate and elevate them within your organization. Add an agenda topic at your next town hall meeting to tell a story about a sponsor who advocated for a protégé and what the outcome was. You can even do this on a smaller scale at your next team meeting. Spotlighting these relationships makes them more accessible to others. It's a great way to give visibility to protégés on the rise and also spotlight the leaders and executives that are living your organization's mission around talent development. They will become a magnet for other diverse talent looking for advocacy and support. It's also an alternative for organizations that might be reluctant to bake in sponsorship as part of a leader's performance evaluation. Various research studies suggest that tying sponsorship to a person's performance or bonus can have both positive and negative impacts. One thing is for certain: sharing broadly across the organization that an executive is modeling the way by sponsoring diverse talent has a ripple effect to others. If other executives see them being championed and celebrated, they will intrinsically understand what the organization values and how the organization is living those values. It can create healthy tension within the organization and demonstrate that performing well financially and operationally is not only what the organization cares about. Creating a following, where employees want to work for you, opens up greater opportunities for leadership within your organization. Celebrate the top sponsors in your organization—people investing in developing the pipeline.

BECOME ACTIVE IN BUSINESS RESOURCE GROUPS (BRGS) TO IDENTIFY DIVERSE TALENT

I believe that to identify diverse talent, you have to gain proximity to diverse talent. You can't expect talent to appear out of nowhere. A good sponsor will go out and seek diverse talent in many different ways. BRGs have grown in popularity as a safe space for employees who have commonalities to congregate and discuss topics that are pertinent to them. Every organization has a variety of BRGs, whether they are focused on the veteran population, Asian Americans, or people with disabilities. Personally, I have been a member of many BRGs, several of which I do not naturally relate to based on who I am. For example, I have joined BRGs for LGBTQ employees because I was curious to learn what the pain points were for their experience in our company. It gave me a broader perspective, and I learned so much about what the journey is like for a lesbian or gay employee in our organization. I also got to meet talented employees in areas of our business in which I do not daily interact. That's the beauty of the BRGs. You can be a member simply because you have interest or passion around the topic or the community. I highly recommend organizations to encourage executives to either attend events put on by different BRGs or become a member themselves. You might find that because the BRG is designed to be a place for all employees to congregate, you will get exposure to talent that you never even knew existed. For example, if you are a white executive and become a member or ally of a BRG for Black males, by design you will gain exposure in a bigger way to existing talent. If there is an opportunity for you to serve as an executive sponsor of a BRG, take that opportunity. If a BRG doesn't exist in your organization, work with your leadership to advocate for one to be launched. Be proactive in creating the environment for executives and leaders to find the diverse talent they are looking for.

ENCOURAGE ATTENDANCE
AT DIVERSITY CONFERENCES

Conference attendance is another great way to identify and uncover underrepresented talent. I have personally found value in networking at conferences, given the number of organizations that attend and the diversity of attendees I have been introduced to. What I've enjoyed most is finding how much I have in common with other attendees and how conferences can supercharge your network. I have both attended and spoken at conferences, and both experiences have expanded my networking circle by giving me access to rising talent as well as senior executives. Organizations should absolutely encourage executive leaders to attend conferences, especially those that have a theme of diversity equity and inclusion. Aside from the fact that attending conferences allows your executives to represent your organization well, it is also a wonderful source of talent. Associations like the National Black MBA Association and others hold annual conferences on topics related to your specific industry as well as on how to find emerging talent (look up some of these themes). Participation by your executive leaders is dually valuable—it's an educational event for them and a way to understand trends impacting your organization. You never know whom you might be sitting with at a conference who could be looking for their next job or their next sponsor.

10

ADVANCING TEN THOUSAND
WOMEN OF COLOR BY 2030

I have always believed in the multiplier effect when it comes to making transformational change. The valiant acts of an individual, when multiplied, can have substantial impacts to changing behavior and changing outcomes. It is the foundation behind my 100x2030 initiative. I knew that there was only so much I could accomplish by making a personal commitment to sponsor women of color. I wanted this commitment to outlive me and to grow and become part of the definition of leadership. Instead of sponsorship being done on the side, when a leader has time, I wanted it to be part of the air leaders breathe. It should be a part of a leader's self-evaluation on how they are developing as executives. I also wanted this initiative to feel like a mutual sense of accountability. The executives and organizations that become part of this initiative should hold each other accountable, share best practices on how sponsorship is evolving for their workforce, and tell compelling stories of women of color who were sponsored and achieved higher levels of success. As I mentioned before, it's all about changing the narrative around how to advance the pipeline of diverse talent through demonstrated outcomes of advocacy and allyship.

Let me pause and take a step back to explain the 100x2030 initiative to you. The pace of change in business requires corporations to think differently about inclusiveness and make better, more informed decisions based on a diversity of perspectives. Future-focused companies will put their people at the center of transformation and place a premium on elevating diverse voices to the table. By creating a more inclusive leadership environment, organizations will be more agile and responsive, strengthen decision making, and take appropriate, time-sensitive risks to position the organization for growth and longevity.

To accomplish this, organizations must diversity their leadership structures and reflect the communities they serve. The 100x2030 initiative inspires inclusive leadership with a specific focus on moving the needle by sponsoring one hundred women of color within this decade. It is more than a personal and professional commitment. It is a career movement designed to amplify the careers of women of color through active sponsorship and advocacy. This global initiative is focused on creating a community of executives, leaders, managers, and organizations that fundamentally believe in the power of sponsorship to advance women of color into senior leadership.

If you are an individual professional intrigued by 100x2030, your commitment is a direct approach to paying it forward and making a measurable impact across all industries, whether higher education, retail, or financial services. You will use your power, influence, and political capital to advance the careers of women of color. If you are a corporation, 100x2030 allows you to play an active role in changing the perceptions of the leadership pipeline—to demystify assumptions around the challenges of advancing women of color in corporate America. Your voice in the industry through contributions of articles and thought leadership on sponsorship demonstrates your commitment to diversity.

The initiative includes three components, each designed to build and create momentum for action. The first part is about making the pledge with intentionality. No pledge is too big or too small. If you are new to sponsorship, think about women of color already in your network who are primed for sponsorship, and commit to sponsoring them. I'll talk a little later in this chapter about specific actions you can take. When you are ready to make your commitment, I ask you to do two things. I want you to sit down with the diverse female protégé you are planning to sponsoring and have a conversation with her. Tell her that you want to be a sponsor for her. Ask her about her career goals and how you can help her achieve them. Talking to your protégé about your commitment makes that commitment real and creates mutual accountability between the two of you. No more silent sponsors. Step into your bravery and let her know that you've got her back. After you have that conversation, I would love to hear about it along with your commitment. Drop me a note at hello@jhaymeetynan.com and let's connect about how you plan to show up as a sponsor. This is regardless of whether you are an individual or an organization making the commitment. I want to have a conversation with you.

The second part is tracking your success. Have any protégés you've sponsored had a powerful and positive outcome? Did a junior executive get the chance to present at a major senior meeting? How did she feel, knowing that she had your sponsorship? Did a diverse female manager finally receive a promotion because you advocated for her in the promotion meeting? We will catalog these collective actions and outcomes so that we will get down to the specifics about what sponsorship looks and feels like. I don't want sponsorship to be theoretical or nebulous. I want it to be something we can all touch and be specific about. These successes will evolve into thought leadership and articles about sponsorship that will help educate leaders on the tactical aspects of sponsoring talent.

The third part of this initiative is the crème de la crème. It's one thing to sponsor protégés. It's quite another to tell these stories publicly. Sharing best practices and stories of sponsorship is a powerful tool to create greater accessibility by spotlighting leaders and their proteges on the power of advocacy and sponsorship. In 2020, I did a pilot of sharing these types of stories on Linkedin, both from protégés I have sponsored and individuals that have made their commitments to sponsor others. It generated significant buzz, with more than thirty thousand views and one thousand comments, just by my posting these inspiring stories for the broader professional community. There was dialogue from LinkedIn users who tagged their sponsors using #100x2030 and shared how their sponsors had accelerated their careers. The conversations were infectious and started to create a sense of community among leaders that share our common belief—that sponsorship is the key to advancing diverse talent.

See figure 10.1 for an example of how the 100x2030 initiative showcases these stories.

100x2030 Stories of Sponsorship (S.O.S)
Scholarships for Women of Color with Peloton Coaching

#100x2030

Figure 10.1. Stories of Sponsorship. *Jhaymee Tynan*

So how do we do this is an intentional and collective way? How do we make the most impact via 100x2030? To me, the equation is simple. My goal with the 100x2030 initiative is that one thousand executives and organizations will make a commitment to sponsor one hundred women of color by 2030. In doing so, we will impact the careers of ten thousand (maybe more) diverse women. You might also be asking yourself, why 2030? Won't this initiative take even more time to gain visibility and inspire leaders toward action? Well, if you're like me, you are exhausted by seeing the same statistics year after year, as they relate to the slow progress of advancing women of color. We cannot keep doing the same things over and over and expect different results. If you ask any research institution about how long it will take for pay equity for diverse women, the answer is that it will take more than one hundred years to reach that goal. And the numbers are continuing to get worse each day. Why not put yourself in the driver's seat of change by using your power and influence and take action now?

ACTIONS YOU CAN TAKE— THE SPECTRUM OF SPONSORSHIP

In reflecting on those horrific statistics about the labor workforce in late 2020, I sat down to write my thoughts about my disappointment and anger regarding how many women had left the workforce. I believed that I had the power within me to sponsor women myself. I didn't want to overthink this commitment. Some leaders feel paralyzed to take actions of sponsorship because it can seem like a daunting task, especially if you equate sponsorship with being able to promote your protégés to the next level. There are so many different ways to sponsor women outside of being able to get them promoted at work that could have influential impact on their trajectory. I felt that there was a spectrum to the actions that sponsors could take based on a couple of factors: their level of comfort and their perceived influence. The spectrum goes along with the evolution of a sponsorship relationship and is categorized by entry-, mid-, and senior-level activities. I intentionally did not categorize these activities based on level

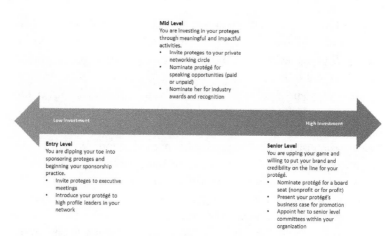

Figure 10.2.   Spectrum of Sponsorship. *Jhaymee Tynan*

of risk. First, I believe that we need to navigate away from thinking of these sorts of advocacy activities as risk-taking endeavors. As I've mentioned previously, risk has a deeply negative connotation, and we need to view sponsorship as a positive behavior to instill in leaders. While it might be true that there is a certain level of risk inherent in sponsorship, practicing these activities as part of your leadership routine will help enrich the sponsorship relationship and grow your comfort with engaging in sponsorship naturally. All of the activities in the spectrum of sponsorship will have a positive impact for your protégé, no matter how big or small (see figure 10.2).

ENTRY LEVEL—DIPPING YOUR
TOE INTO SPONSORSHIP

Everyone is on their own journey when it comes to being a leader, and the same goes for sponsorship. Perhaps you've never viewed yourself as a sponsor, or maybe you've felt that you needed permission to be an active sponsor. Whatever your reasoning, let's throw away those thoughts and think about how to get started as a sponsor. I call these entry-level or small acts of sponsorship. They may be small, but these actions will have a big impact in the mind of your protégé. These actions are all designed to help you practice sponsorship in your leadership routine while giving broader visibility within your organization to your protégé. The more visibility your protégé gets with your peers and a broader audience, the more it increases their confidence so that they can be successful but also shows them that you are willing to support them through your sponsorship.

Actions include:

- Support your protégé's ideas in high-visibility meetings.
- Invite your protégé to your senior-level meetings.
- Introduce your protégé to a few high profile executives in your network.
- Learn about your protégé's value proposition, and share talking points about your protégé's accomplishments regularly with peers.
- Advocate for worker of color workplace flexibility.

MID-LEVEL—COMMITTING TO DEEPER ACTION

Let's say you've been a sponsor before, but your actions haven't resulted in the type of impact you were hoping to make for your protégé. Or perhaps you are aware of your power and influence, and you'd like to make an even bigger commitment for your protégé that will result in positive outcomes faster. You're ready to make a deeper investment in your advocacy. These tangible, mid-level activities allow you to do just that—accelerate your commitment through bigger actions.

Actions include:

- Invite your protégé into your private networking circle.
- Nominate her for executive-development programs.
- Nominate your protégé for industry awards and recognition.

- Nominate her for speaking opportunities at major conferences.
- Serve as a credible reference for her for job opportunities.
- Pay for her membership in exclusive professional networking circles.

SENIOR LEVEL—UPPING YOUR GAME

These are the types of activities that most professionals associate sponsorship with and that have traditionally had the biggest impact on career development. These are the stories where you'll hear a diverse professional getting their first executive promotion or getting on a high-visibility committee within their organization as a direct result of you placing her there. These are activities that we should as sponsors aspire to, but also require the right positional power and influence to achieve successfully. If you are ready and willing to take these actions, please do. As you become more senior in your career, these actions may feel more achievable and organic to you. But don't let these types of actions scare you as a sponsor, based on where you are in your career journey. Again, do a self-assessment—do you have the ability to make good on these actions based on your commitment to the protégé, the depth of your network, and the strength of your political and social capital?

Actions include:

- Present your protégé's business case for promotion.
- Promote her to an executive level or people-management position.
- Ask her to present your organization's business results at the next board meeting.
- Appoint her to senior-level committees (Audit, Nominating, Board Chair position).
- Invest and sponsor her for a national board preparation program.
- Nominate your protégé for a board seat (nonprofit or for profit).

PRACTICE MAKES PERFECT

As a leader, you should consider any act on the spectrum as a demonstration of your ability and commitment to sponsor others. Figure out what feels natural to you and what you feel most comfortable with. Ideally, I would love all sponsors to be working their way up the spectrum to have the biggest impact on the careers of their protégés. But everyone needs to start at a place that is best for them. This is the core of creating your sponsorship practice. Using the spectrum of sponsorship is a great approach to modeling the way for your peers and your superiors to incorporate sponsorship into how they lead every day. Practice makes perfect. The more you practice these acts of sponsorship, the more it becomes second nature to you and becomes part of your brand as a leader. Those around you can point to specific instances of the impact you have on creating the next generation of leadership. And there is intrinsic value in being able to support the advancement of women in your organization. It simply feels good to serve in the best interest of your protégé. Acts of sponsorship are contagious, and you'll find that other leaders will step into their courage when they see you actively engaging in advancing women. In my sponsorship practice, I do a lot of journaling. I'm the type of person who loves to reflect on my thoughts and feelings often. Have you ever considered journaling about the experience of one of the protégés you've sponsored? What was the situation they came to you for? How did you show up as a sponsor? What was the active sponsorship on the spectrum that you decided to take on their behalf? What was the outcome? I highly encourage all leaders to consider writing down their sponsorship journey, either as the sponsor or the protégé.

EPILOGUE

In reflecting on my journey to write this book, I am reinvigorated by the acts of sponsorship I have witnessed each day over the past year. Leaders didn't even realize they were stepping into sponsorship. The small acts of sponsorship, whether a colleague amplifying and championing a women's article published in a major journal and sharing it via social media or providing a positive review on a female leader's latest conference presentation, have inspired me in new ways. They have also reinforced to me that in general, we want to support one another. We want to see more women on stage sharing their latest research or more female entrepreneurs breaking out on their own and launching new products. Perhaps the pandemic shifted something in all of us, shifted our thinking that succeeding in business is not about competition, but collaboration and cooperation. Maybe the fatigue related to the lack of diversity in leadership and racial events in the United States has not only settled in but ignited a fire in all of us to *do better* and *be better*. The pandemic has certainly given me time to reflect on the impact and legacy I want to make as an executive; and simply achieving success without paying it forward is no longer a focus of mine. To me, there's no sense in working hard and climbing the corporate ladder if there is no one behind for me to lift as I climb. Simply put, I believe that there are infinite opportunities for success, as many as, if not more than, the number of stars in the sky. What if each woman of color had the opportunity to be her own star?

Solving the challenges of diversity in leadership does not have t be an insurmountable task. It requires motivation, conviction, ` general aptitude to not only do what is right but to have th⸀

to advocate in the service of others. The data speaks for itself—in business, we do not have enough diverse leaders that represent the communities and the people whom we seek to serve. Diversity programs are not enough. Posting a black square on Instagram in solidarity against racism is certainly not enough. Making sweeping statements about your organization's commitment to diversity is not going to move the needle. We as leaders must be willing to transition from rhetoric to measurable action. And if we are not seeing tangible results, we must treat diversity in leadership as a business problem. We move to corrective action. We expect more from our executives and build better competencies around inclusive leadership and cultural competency into our leadership expectations, frameworks, and training. We evaluate leaders on their readiness for promotion based on what diverse talent they've developed and elevated during their tenure. And we simply do not rest until we see leadership reflect the world we live in from gender-, race-, and sexual-orientation perspectives.

I believe that accelerating diversity in leadership comes down to three important things. First, you and your organization must believe that diverse representation begins at the top by modeling the way every day. Without these behaviors, strategy, and growth, business results will continue to suffer, and your organization will lose competitive advantage and become obsolete. Second, you must believe that you have a role in being part of the solution, based on your privilege as a leader and executive. You are in a position of accountability and trust. When you occupy spaces that your diverse protégés do not, you advocate for their representation. When you see opportunities to extend your network to a rising Black or Brown female, so that she may expand or develop her own network, you don't hesitate. You make the warm introduction. You follow up to ensure that the conversation went well and offer other ways to assist. If a protégé makes a mistake as she is developing her sponsor readiness, you extend grace. You take your leadership position as a cultivator and connector of talent. You fill the leadership pipeline and ensure that diverse talent in the pipeline emerges to senior leadership. Third, you must believe that you achieved your success because someone else gave you wings to fly. Whether it was a mentor, sponsor, coach, or ally (or all four), there was someone that saw potential in you and created or orchestrated moves that allowed you to be promoted. You were provided safe spaces to fail, to get up, and try again. You were introduced by a friend to that senior executive that put you on your first strategy project, which you delivered and for which you were celebrated for your thought leadership and point of view. You were forgiven when you bombed at that presentation to the president of your business unit and given an opportunity to make things right. Your public and silent sponsors have been there every step of the way making sure that the pathway for you was flanked by bumper lanes so that you'd eventually hit that strike. All of the support you've had most likely is not the same for women of color in the workplace. Her wings may have been clipped, as she had to deal with being labeled as angry, a troublemaker, or difficult to work with simply because she's advocating for herself. Instead, help her fly. Be her sponsor. Advocate for her.

According to the Center for American Progress, Black and Hispanic women in the United States are not projected to reach pay parity with white men until 2133 and 2220, respectively.[1] These numbers are even far worse in countries across the globe. While pay parity will be achieved long after this book is published and certainly after I've lived my life, that doesn't mean we should wait to take action now. Not only should we be sponsoring women of color in career advancement, but we should also advocate for equal pay for her on that journey. No more disparities in how we value the work of women of color versus her white colleagues. No more excuses on why a Hispanic female VP should be paid less than a white female VP with the same job description. Transparency and fairness in compensation should be part of sponsorship, and I commend the executives and leaders that always think about and advocate fair pay for their diverse colleagues.

I will end with this thought. When you view equity and equality as a zero-sum game, you will always lose. Winning the war on talent requires you to believe that building a bigger table of opportunities allows all parties to win. It costs you nothing to send those invitations to the table. As James Keller puts it, "A candle loses nothing by lighting another candle."

NOTES

CHAPTER 1. YOU NEED TO CALM DOWN

1. Shelby Livingston, "Racism Is Still a Problem in the C-Suite," *Modern Healthcare*, February 24, 2018, https://www.modernhealthcare.com/article/20180224/NEWS/180229948/racism-still-a-problem-in-healthcare-s-c-suite.

2. "Women in the Workplace 2019." McKinsey and LeanIn.org, accessed November 4, 2020, https://www.mckinsey.com/featured-insights/gender-equality/women-in-the-workplace-2019.

CHAPTER 2. A RECKONING IS HERE

1. Annalyn Kurtz, "The US Economy Lost 140,000 Jobs in December. All of Them Were Held by Women," CNN, accessed January 11, 2021, https://www.cnn.com/2021/01/08/economy/women-job-losses-pandemic/index.html.

2. Anne Branigin, "The Pandemic Set Women's Equality Back Another Generation, New Report Says," The Lily, accessed April 8, 2021, https://www.thelily.com/the-pandemic-set-womens-equality-back-another-generation-a-new-report-says/.

3. "Women in the Workplace 2021," McKinsey and LeanIn.org, accessed October 30, 2021, https://www.mckinsey.com/featured-insights/diversity-and-inclusion/women-in-the-workplace.

4. "Women in the Workplace 2021."

5. "Women in the Workplace 2021."

6. Stephanie Mehta, "Billie Jean King-Backed Study Finds Women of Color Feel Undervalued at Work," *Fast Company*, accessed November 28,

2021, https://www.fastcompany.com/90697122/billie-jean-king-backed -study-finds-women-of-color-feel-undervalued-at-work.

7. Mehta, "Billie Jean King-Backed Study."

8. Courtney Connley, "More than 1 in 3 Black Women Are on the Front Lines of the Pandemic, but They Aren't Even Close to Equal Pay," CNBC, accessed July 2, 2021, https://www.cnbc.com/2020/08/13/black -women-are-on-the-front-lines-of-the-pandemic-but-they-arent-even -close-to-equal-pay.html.

9. Teresa Perez, "Sponsors: Valuable Allies Not Everyone Has," Payscale, July 31, 2019, https://www.payscale.com/research-and-insights /mentorship-sponsorship-benefits/.

10. Lucy Erickson, PhD, "The Disproportionate Impact of COVID-19 on Women of Color," Society for Women's Health Research, accessed April 12, 2021, https://swhr.org/the-disproportionate-impact-of-covid-19-on -women-of-color/.

11. Khristopher J. Brooks, "Why Many Black Employees Don't Want to Return to the Office," CBS News, accessed November 1, 2021, https:// www.cbsnews.com/news/black-workers-return-to-office-future-forum -workplace/.

CHAPTER 3. IT'S NOT A PIPELINE ISSUE

1. Sonia Thompson, "Despite Being the Most Educated, Black Women Earn Less Money at Work, in Entrepreneurship, and in Venture Capital. Here Are Three Ways to Fix it," *Inc.*, accessed May 7, 2021, https://www .inc.com/sonia-thompson/Black-women-equal-pay-equity-how-to-make -progress.html.

2. "Degrees Conferred by Race and Sex: Fast Facts," National Center for Education Statistics, accessed May 9, 2021, https://nces.ed.gov/fastfacts /display.asp?id=72.

3. "Black Women to Reach Pay Equity with White Men in 2130," Institute for Women's Policy Research, accessed August 4, 2021, https:// iwpr.org/iwpr-issues/esme/black-women-to-reach-equal-pay-with-white -white-men-in-2130/.

4. Ruth Umoh, "75% of Senior Execs Say They'd Leave Their Company for One That Values Diversity," CNBC, updated July 26, 2017, https:// www.cnbc.com/2017/07/26/75-percent-of-execs-would-leave-their-com pany-for-one-that-values-diversity.html.

5. Grace Donnelly, "Only 3% of Fortune 500 Companies Share Full Diversity Data," *Fortune,* accessed June 3, 2021, https://finance.yahoo.com/news/only-3-fortune-500-companies-122544386.html.

6. Leanne Italie, "Dictionary.com Names 'Allyship' Its 2021 Word of the Year, Despite Just Being Added," Associated Press, accessed December 14, 2021, https://www.usatoday.com/story/news/nation/2021/12/06/dictionary-com-allyship-2021-word/6408641001/.

CHAPTER 4. SPONSORSHIP LOOKS DIFFERENT FOR WOMEN OF COLOR

1. Stephanie Bradley Smith, "How a Lack of Sponsorship Keeps Black Women Out of the C-Suite," *Harvard Business Review*, accessed October 2, 2021, https://hbr.org/2021/03/how-a-lack-of-sponsorship-keeps-black-women-out-of-the-c-suite.

2. Jill, interview.

3. Layla, interview.

4. Anika, interview.

CHAPTER 5. POWER DYNAMICS IN SPONSORSHIP

1. Doug, interview.

2. Karyn Heath, Jill Flynn, Mary Davis Holt, and Diana Faison, *The Influence Effect: A New Path to Power for Women Leaders* (Berrett-Koehler Publishers, 2017).

3. Nicole, interview.

4. "Women in the Workplace 2021," McKinsey and LeanIn.org, accessed November 17, 2021, https://wiw-report.s3.amazonaws.com/Women_in_the_Workplace_2021.pdf.

CHAPTER 6. THE SPONSORSHIP MANIFESTO

1. Amanda Chan, "7 Science Backed Reasons Why Generosity Is Good for Your Health," Huffington Post, accessed July 19, 2021, https://www.huffpost.com/entry/generosity-health_n_4323727.

2. Ashley, interview.

3. "Women in the Workplace 2019," McKinsey and LeanIn.org, accessed September 18, 2021, https://www.mckinsey.com/featured-insights/gender-equality/women-in-the-workplace-2019.

CHAPTER 8. SPONSOR READINESS
FOR WOMEN OF COLOR

1. Sharon Melnick, PhD, *Success under Stress: Powerful Tools for Staying Calm, Confident, and Productive When the Pressure's On* (AMACOM, 2013).
2. Tatiana Walk-Morris, "Employers and Co-Workers Want Black Women's Expertise. But Are They Paying Them for It?," *The Guardian*, accessed December 10, 2021, https://www.theguardian.com/us-news/2020/nov/06/employers-and-co-workers-want-black-womens-expertise-but-are-they-paying-them-for-it.

CHAPTER 9. CREATING AN
INCLUSIVE SPONSORSHIP CULTURE

1. "Developing Organizational Leaders," Society for Human Resource Management, accessed September 20, 2021, https://www.shrm.org/resourcesandtools/tools-and-samples/toolkits/pages/developingorganizationalleaders.aspx.

EPILOGUE

1. Robin Bleiweis, Jocelyn Frye, and Rose Khattar, "Women of Color and the Wage Gap," Center for American Progress, November 17, 2021, https://www.americanprogress.org/article/women-of-color-and-the-wage-gap/.

BIBLIOGRAPHY

"Black Women to Reach Pay Equity with White Men in 2130." Institute for Women's Policy Research, accessed August 4, 2021, https://iwpr.org /iwpr-issues/esme/black-women-to-reach-equal-pay-with-white-white -men-in-2130/.

Bleiweis, Robin, Frye, Jocelyn, and Khattar, Rose. "Women of Color and the Wage Gap." Center for American Progress, November 17, 2021, https://www.americanprogress.org/article/women-of-color-and-the -wage-gap/.

Bradley Smith, Stephanie. "How a Lack of Sponsorship Keeps Black Women Out of the C-Suite." *Harvard Business Review*, accessed October 2, 2021, https://hbr.org/2021/03/how-a-lack-of-sponsorship-keeps -black-women-out-of-the-c-suite.

Brooks, Khristopher J. "Why Many Black Employees Don't Want to Return to the Office." *CBS News*, accessed November 1, 2021, https:// www.cbsnews.com/news/black-workers-return-to-office-future-forum -workplace/.

Connley, Courtney. "More than 1 in 3 Black Women Are on the Front Lines of the Pandemic, but They Aren't Even Close to Equal Pay," CNBC, accessed July 2, 2021, https://www.cnbc.com/2020/08/13 /black-women-are-on-the-front-lines-of-the-pandemic-but-they-arent -even-close-to-equal-pay.html.

"Degrees Conferred by Race and Sex: Fast Facts." National Center for Education Statistics, accessed May 9, 2021, https://nces.ed.gov/fastfacts /display.asp?id=72.

"Developing Organizational Leaders." Society for Human Resource Management, accessed September 20, 2021, https://www.shrm.org /resourcesandtools/tools-and-samples/toolkits/pages/developingorgani zationalleaders.aspx.

Donnelly, Grace. "Only 3% of Fortune 500 Companies Share Full Diversity Data." *Fortune*, accessed June 3, 2021, https://finance.yahoo.com/news/only-3-fortune-500-companies-122544386.html.

Erickson, Lucy. "The Disproportionate Impact of COVID-19 on Women of Color," Society for Women's Health Research, accessed April 12, 2021, https://swhr.org/the-disproportionate-impact-of-covid-19-on-women-of-color/.

Heath, Karen, Flynn, Jill, Holt, Mary Davis, and Faison, Diana. *The Influence Effect: A New Path to Power for Women Leaders* (Berrett-Koehler Publishers, 2017).

Italie, Leanne. "Dictionary.com Names 'Allyship' Its 2021 Word of the Year, Despite Just Being Added," Associated Press, accessed December 14, 2021, https://www.usatoday.com/story/news/nation/2021/12/06/dictionary-com-allyship-2021-word/6408641001/.

LeanIn.org. "The State of Black Women in Corporate America," accessed November 5, 2020, https://media.sgff.io/sgff_r1eHetbDYb/2020-08-13/1597343917539/Lean_In_-_State_of_Black_Women_in_Corporate_America_Report_1.pdf.

Livingston, Shelby. "Racism Is Still a Problem in the C-Suite." *Modern Healthcare*, February 24, 2018, https://www.modernhealthcare.com/article/20180224/NEWS/180229948/racism-still-a-problem-in-healthcare-s-c-suite.

McKinsey and LeanIn.org. "Women in the Workplace 2019," accessed November 4, 2020, https://www.mckinsey.com/featured-insights/gender-equality/women-in-the-workplace-2019.

McKinsey and LeanIn.org. "Women in the Workplace 2021," accessed October 30, 2021, https://www.mckinsey.com/featured-insights/diversity-and-inclusion/women-in-the-workplace.

Mehta, Stephanie. "Billie Jean King-Backed Study Finds Women of Color Feel Undervalued at Work," *Fast Company*, accessed November 28, 2021, https://www.fastcompany.com/90697122/billie-jean-king-backed-study-finds-women-of-color-feel-undervalued-at-work.

Melnick, Sharon. *Success under Stress: Powerful Tools for Staying Calm, Confident, and Productive When the Pressure's On* (AMACOM, 2013).

O'Brien, Sarah. "Here's How the Wage Gap Affects Black Women," CNBC, August 22, 2019, https://www.cnbc.com/2019/08/22/heres-how-the-gender-wage-gap-affects-this-minority-group.html.

Perez, Teresa. "Sponsors: Valuable Allies Not Everyone Has," *Payscale*, July 31, 2019, https://www.payscale.com/research-and-insights/mentorship -sponsorship-benefits/.

Thompson, Sonia. "Despite Being the Most Educated, Black Women Earn Less Money at Work, in Entrepreneurship, and in Venture Capital. Here Are Three Ways to Fix it," *Inc.*, accessed May 7, 2021, https://www.inc .com/sonia-thompson/Black-women-equal-pay-equity-how-to-make -progress.html.

Umoh, Ruth. "75% of Senior Execs Say They'd Leave Their Company for One That Values Diversity," CNBC, updated July 26, 2017, https:// www.cnbc.com/2017/07/26/75-percent-of-execs-would-leave-their -company-for-one-that-values-diversity.html.

Walk-Morris, Tatiana. "Employers and Co-Workers Want Black Women's Expertise. But Are They Paying Them for It?" *The Guardian*, accessed December 10, 2021, https://www.theguardian.com/us-news/2020/nov/06 /employers-and-co-workers-want-black-womens-expertise-but-are-they -paying-them-for-it.

INDEX

ABOUT THE AUTHOR

Jhaymee Tynan is a leadership advisor at a global talent and executive search firm. In her role, she provides executive search and leadership advisory services for senior executives of healthcare services, pharmaceuticals, and life sciences organizations. Previously, Jhaymee was enterprise assistant vice president, integration at Atrium Health, an academic healthcare system where she led multi-billion-dollar post-merger integrations for health system mergers and acquisitions (M&A) across the Southeast. She was also a manager at Deloitte Consulting, focused on business model transformation in healthcare.

She is also the founder of 100x2030, a career initiative that aims to increase representation for women of color at the senior-executive levels of healthcare organizations globally. She inspires executives and corporations to make commitments of sponsorship. Currently, Jhaymee has commitments to sponsor more than six hundred women of color, with a goal of impacting ten thousand women by 2030.

A seasoned executive with a passion for bringing people and organizations together, she is frequently tapped to present on topics including change management, emotional intelligence, the future of leadership, and creating organizational value. She has presented for respected organizations such as the American Medical Association, American College of Healthcare Executives, HealthLeaders Media, HLTH, Modern Healthcare, Northwestern University, Kaiser Permanente, Froedtert Health, and Becker's Healthcare. She also regularly creates content and writes blogs on strategy and leadership on her website (www.jhaymeetynan.com).

In addition to her full-time roles, Jhaymee has served on the board of directors for the American Hospital Association's Society for Healthcare Strategy and Market Development, a national professional association with over four thousand members focused on strategic planning, business development, communications, and public relations. She served on the Nominating Committee and will serve on the Executive Strategies Committee in 2021. She also serves on the global board of directors for the Healthcare Businesswomen's Association, an international nonprofit with over ten thousand members, designed to advance gender parity for women in the business of healthcare.

She has received numerous industry awards for her work in healthcare strategy and M&A and for championing sponsorship for women of color, including *Modern Healthcare*'s Top 25 Emerging Leaders, *Becker's Healthcare* 70 African American Leaders in Healthcare to Know, *Diversity MBA's* Top 100 Executives under 50, *Charlotte Business Journal*'s 40 under 40, and *Bizwomen's* Headliners in Healthcare.

Jhaymee holds a BS in finance from Virginia Tech, an MS in project management from The George Washington University, and an MBA from the Goizueta Business School at Emory University. She is also board certified in healthcare management as a fellow by the American College of Healthcare Executives. She enjoys spending time with her family, writing, and exploring new cultures with her husband and two fur-babies, Agnes and Kenji.